Translated from the Ja
Originally published in 1992 by Japan Broadcast Put
under the title (translated) *Woven Beadw*
English translation: Co
Cover design and layout: Yasuko Shi
Photography: Masayuki Tsutsui
Stylist: Shouko Nakayasu
Instructions: Chikami Okuda, Chihiro Tsushima
Tracing: Kiyoshi Suzuki, Susumu Yatagai
Editor: Mamiko Shibasaki

Delica Beads provided by: Miyuki Trading Co.

English language edition published by
LACIS PUBLICATIONS
3163 Adeline Street
Berkeley, CA 94703

ISBN 0-916896-98-6
Printed in China

Wild Roses

◆

Beads are woven, one by one, in the way an artist creates a painting, to form this classic pattern. The background is worked in lustrous cream-colored beads, which accentuate the flower pattern.

Oval Brooch (A)
Instructions on page 49

Tyrolean Ribbon Brooch
Instructions on page 49

Square-Cut Brooch
Instructions on page 50

Oval Brooch (B)
Instructions on page 50

accessories with miniature flowers

Flowered Hat Brooch
Instructions: Page 51

Draped Ribbon Barrette
Instructions: Page 51

Garlands

For the barrette and brooches, we used transparent beads woven on beige thread to produce a brilliance reminiscent of crystal. For the two flower pendants, we used a cream-colored background, which adds a touch of elegance.

Treble Clef Brooch
Instructions: Page 52

Diamond Pendant
Instructions: Page 52

Round Pendant
Instructions: Page 53

5

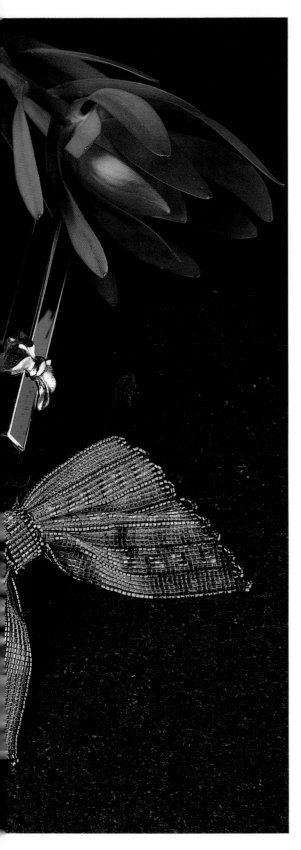

Hair Ornaments with Miniature Roses

◆

We used the same transparent beads for these pieces, but when they are woven on black thread, they glitter like the wings of a cicada.

Hair Band
Instructions: Page 53

Ribbon Barrette
Instructions: Page 54

Ruched Hair Ornament
Instructions: Page 55

Draped Ribbon Barrette
Instructions: Page 51

accessories with miniature flowers

Bouquets

◆

Weaving these flower motifs on
a black background produces a
beautiful, antique effect.

Round Pendant
Instructions: Page 53

Square Brooch
Instructions: Page 55

Small Triangular Bag
Instructions: Page 56

accessories with miniature flowers

Rose Garden

◆

These antique-style accessories
(a case, a barrette, and a
brooch) are woven in patterns
featuring large or small roses,
and were designed to resemble
petit point.

Petit Point Case
Instructions: Page 58

Oval Brooch (A)
Instructions: Page 49

Ribbon Barrette
Instructions: Page 60

accessories with miniature flowers

Emblems

◆

These emblems look especially striking when worn on the lapel of a tailored jacket.

Shooting Star Emblem
Instructions: Page 61

Flag Emblem
Instructions: Page 62

Flower Garden Emblem
Instructions: Page 63

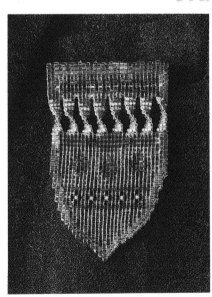

Ruby Emblem
Instructions: Page 63

Sapphire Emblem
Instructions: Page 62

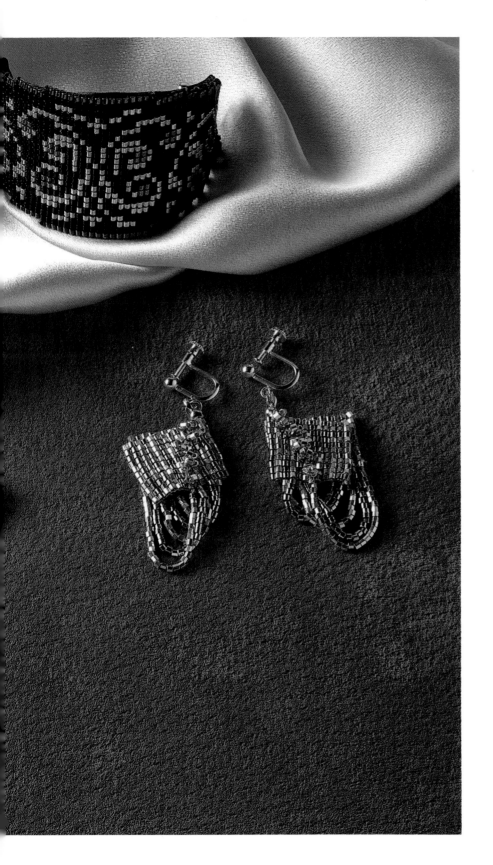

Metallics

◆

These accessories, created
using a variety of techniques
(fringe, loops, and picots),
look marvelous when
woven with metallic beads.

Brooch
Instructions: Page 46

Bracelet with Miniature Flowers (A)
Instructions: Page 48

Loop Brooch
Instructions: Page 65

Semicircular Barrette
Instructions: Page 64

Loop Earrings
Instructions: Page 65

Irises

◆

These pieces feature simple patterns ¾ silver beads on black backgrounds. The striking iris motif is woven symmetrically.

Fringed Brooch
Instructions: Page 65

Square-Cut Brooch
Instructions: Page 66

Ribbon Brooch
Instructions: Page 66

jewels

Monotones

◆

Since these accessories have a rather plain design, we have enhanced the subtle colors with metallic beads, which add a wonderful luster.

Pendant
Instructions: Page 40

Necklace
Instructions: Page 67

Earrings
Instructions: Page 67

Hair Band
Instructions: Page 68

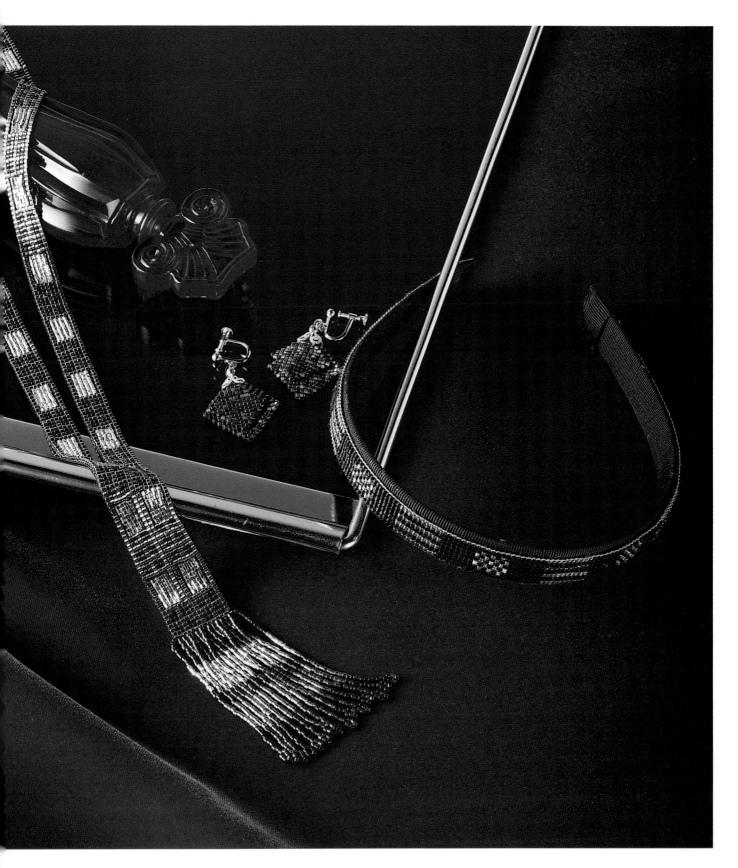

Silver

◆

These pieces were made using a
new style of weaving that creates
a stripe on each row. The
appearance of the bag, bracelet,
and necklace will change in fasci-
nating ways, depending on how
the light shines upon them.

Bag
Instructions: Page 68

Bracelet
Instructions: Page 69

Necklace
Instructions: Page 69

Jewels

Bracelet with Miniature Flowers (B)
Instructions: Page 48

Necklace with Miniature Flowers
Instructions: Page 48

Openwork Bag
Instructions: Page 70

Antique Motifs

◆

These accessories are woven by hand, using traditional
techniques.   Metallic beads add beautiful accents to the
antique look.

jewels

Small Accessories

◆

Even when you use the same technique, you
can create lovely accessories with a three-
dimensional look by varying the form.

Miniature Purse Brooch
Instructions: Page 45

Silk Kerchief Brooch
Instructions: Page 72

jewels

Evening Primrose Barrette
Instructions: Page 71

Evening Primrose Earrings
Instructions: Page 71

Cherry Barrette
Instructions: Page 72

Cherry Earrings
Instructions: Page 72

Double Cherry Blossoms

◆

The metallic sheen of woven bead-work is surprisingly well suited to traditional Japanese patterns. The matching bag and barrette have a cherry-blossom motif.

Bag
Instructions: Page 73

Barrette
Instructions: Page 74

Kaleidoscope

◆

These beautiful, lustrous
hair ornaments are remi-
niscent of Saga brocade,
and look wonderful with
formal attire.

Chignon Cover
Instructions: Page 74

Two Tortoise-Shell Barrettes
Instructions: Page 75

Dreams

◆

You can create pieces using Nishijin brocade colors, or produce a completely different effect by using metallic gold or silver bugle beads.

Stardust Barrette
Instructions: Page 77

Nishijin Brocade Barrette
Instructions: Page 76

Silverwork Barrette
Instructions: Page 77

Gold and Silverwork Brooches
Instructions: Page 78

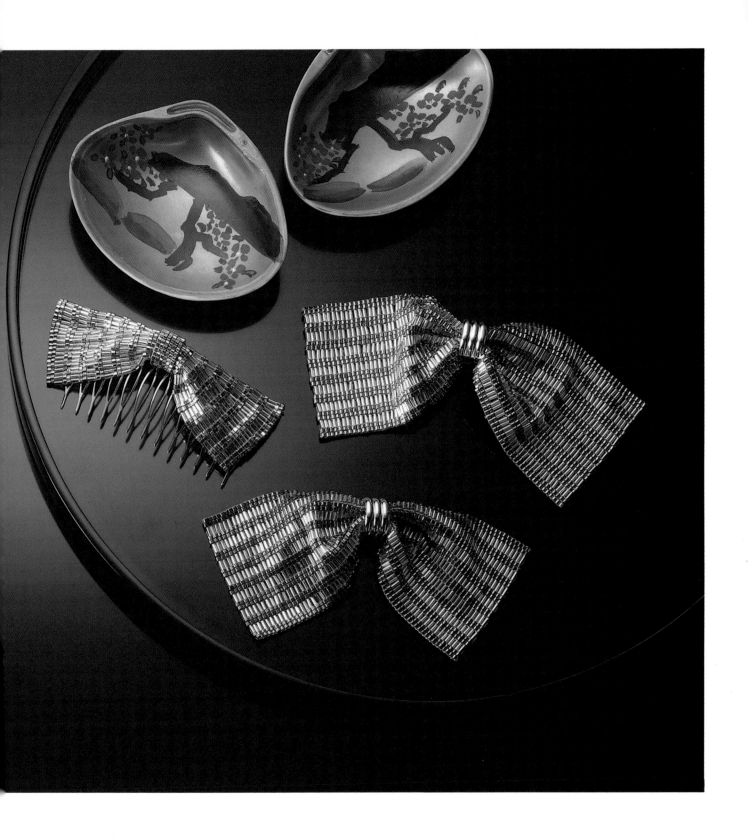

Twilight

◆

This bag, with its oriental colors, and elegant design, goes
well with both Western and Eastern attire.

Afternoon Bag
Instructions: Page 79

32

BASIC BEADWEAVING INSTRUCTIONS
&
INSTRUCTIONS FOR MAKING
THE ACCESSORIES SHOWN IN
THIS BOOK

Miniature Bag with Roses
Instructions: Page 78

In the photographs in this section, we have altered the type of thread to make the illustrations clearer, and decreased the number of warp (vertical) threads. The finished size stated for each piece is merely a benchmark. The numbers in parentheses following the bead colors are color code numbers. "C" indicates cut beads.

● GLASS BEADS FOR WEAVING

CYLINDRICAL AND CUT BEADS

BUGLE BEADS

GLASS BEADS

CYLINDRICAL AND CUT BEADS

These are small glass beads (1 mm long x 1.2 mm dia.). There are two types, cylindrical and cut beads. The holes in them are larger than those in other types of beads, so that the needle can pass through them easily. They come in 170 colors, including transparent, and metallic finish beads. They have a luster that adds a dewy look to a finished piece.

BUGLE BEADS

These beads are longer than cylindrical or cut beads, and are faceted. They have large holes and come in several sizes (e.g., 3 mm, 6 mm, 9 mm), and in approximately 30 colors. Some have a gold, silver, pearl, or matte finish.

● PICKING UP BEADS

Place beads in small boxes, one for each color. To pick them up, place your needle in the box and maneuver it, using a scooping motion.

● WEAVING THREADS

Use sturdy, non-elastic thread; we recommend No. B or C nylon. In most cases, gray thread is used. However, you may wish to use other colors on occasion. Since the thread color influences the appearance of the finished piece, you can obtain interesting effects by varying it.

FINDINGS

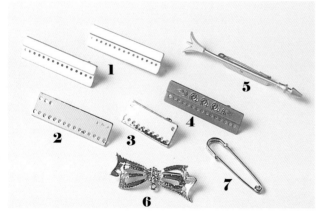

1 Pin back (4.5 cm); **2** Flush perforated pin back (4.5 cm); **3** Flush perforated pin back (3 cm); **4** Pin back with flower pattern (4.5 cm); **5** Arrow-shaped pin back; **6** Ribbon pin; **7** Kilt pin

1 & **2** Bow crimpers; **3** Three-strand clasp; **4** Earring backs; **5** Perforated earring clips.

● LOOMS

SMALL
Spring width: 3"; used to weave small accessories, e.g., pins and necklaces.

MEDIUM
Spring width: 8"; used to weave medium-sized pieces, e.g., purses and bags, etc.

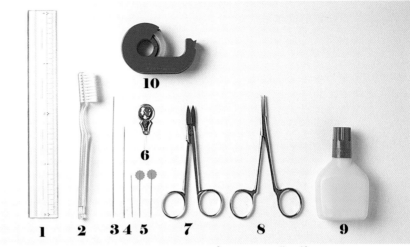

LARGE
Spring width: 11"; used to make larger pieces, e.g. handbags, tapestries, etc.

● OTHER TOOLS

1-Ruler; **2**-Toothbrush (for separating warp threads; use one with dense bristles; **3**-Beading needles (available in three sizes: 2", 3.5" & 5"; **4**-Sewing needle (for joining Sewing needle (for joining woven pieces and attaching findings); **5**-Marking pins; **6**-Needle threader; **7**-Scissors; **8**-Forceps; **9**-Carpenter's glue (choose one that becomes transparent when it dries); **10**-Cellophane tape; You will also need a work board.

● GAUGE

Used for cutting the required length of thread; cut two pieces of plywood or cardboard to the following measurements: 2" wide x 12" long.

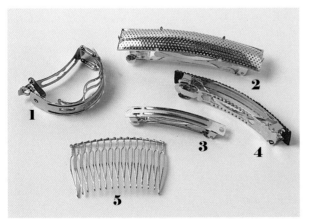

1-Semicircular barrette back; **2**-Perforated barrette back (3"); **3**-Small barrette back (2"); **4**-Large barrette back (3"); **5**-Comb (2-1/4")

1-Chain; **2**-Bail; **3**-Jump ring; **4**-Bead tip; **5**-Bead cap

Large/Small Styrofoam balls (used to make pompoms); large-1" dia.; small-3/4" dia.

Use either a small or medium-sized loom. Warp the loom after you have cut all the threads to the proper length. A good benchmark to use for thread length is the length of finished piece + 30 cm.

This method is recommended when you are weaving a wide piece (a bag or a tapestry), or a long piece (a belt).

★ *For the names of the parts of the loom and instructions for attaching weft threads, see Pages 38 and 39.*

● PREPARING THE WARP THREADS

1 - Cut the two gauges so that they measure half the required thread length. Tape threads to gauge to hold them in place. Wind thread around gauge, and cut it at the top.

● STRINGING THE WARP THREADS

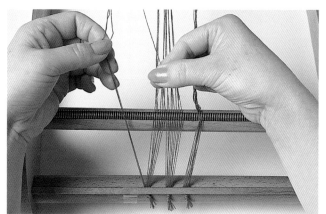

1 - Place threads at the center of the warp beam about 1.5 cm apart. The knots should be at the base of the warp locking bar. Secure the warp locking bar with tape.

2 - Thread each bundle on the spring coils, starting at the center. Tape threads down to secure them.

5 - Place tape over the warp threads on the spring. Pull the threads taut, lay them on the warp beam, and place the warp locking bar on top of them. Tape the warp locking bar to the warp beam.

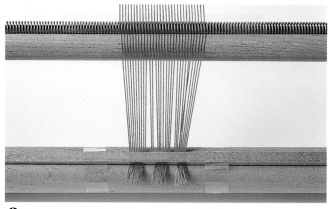

6 - Cut the ends of the threads evenly, leaving 1 cm.

2 - Cut the ends of the threads evenly, leaving 1 cm.

3 - Separate threads into bundles of 10 strands each, and tie them together 1 cm from the end. You will need one more warp thread than the number of beads in the horizontal rows.

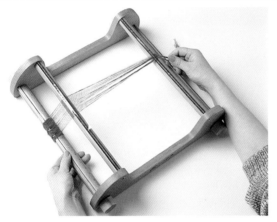

3 - Loosen the warp beam release knob, and wind the warp beam, keeping the threads taut by pulling on them with your other hand; leave about 20 cm of thread.

4 - Turn the loom around, place the warp threads on the other spring, and tie the ends in bundles of 10 strands. Use a toothbrush to align the threads, and place them between the coils of the spring.

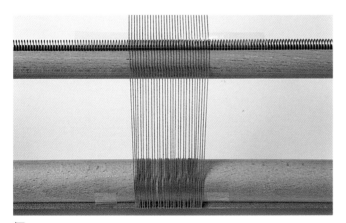

7 - Adjust the tension by winding the warp beam toward you one-and-a-half times; tighten the warp beam release knob.

8 - Tie a weft thread to the leftmost warp thread (see instructions on Page 38).

STRINGING THE WARP THREADS
Warping Method B

With this method, used on a small or medium-sized loom, the warp threads are connected, end to end. We recommend using it when you are weaving small pieces.

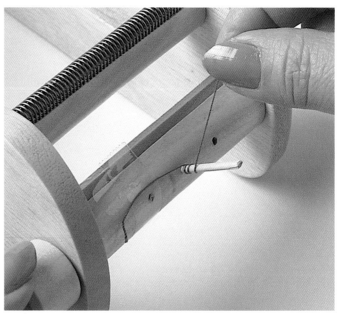

1 - Insert a warp peg into the hole in the warp beam nearest you. Fasten the ends of the threads to the left of the warp beam with tape. Wind the thread around the warp peg three times.

5 - String one more warp thread than number of beads on horizontal rows. End at warp peg nearest you, wrapping thread around it 3 times.

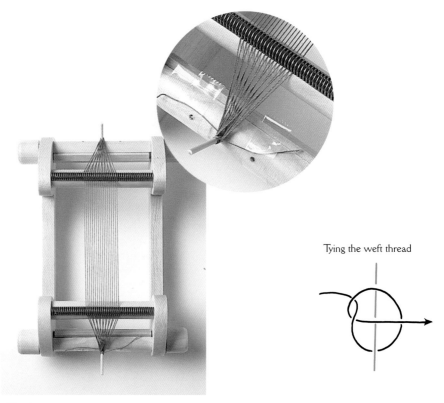

6 - Cut thread, and tape the end to the right of the warp beam.

Tying the weft thread

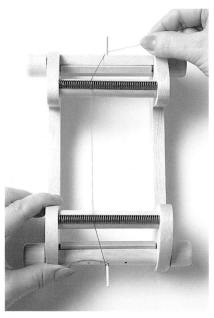

2 - Insert the thread from Step **1** into a coil of the spring at the left side of the loom. Pass it through a coil at the other end of the loom and wind it around the other warp peg.

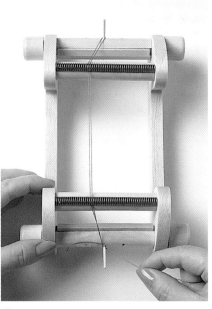

3 - Bring the thread back toward you, passing it through the coil to the right of the coil through which you passed the first thread in Step **2**, and onto the warp peg nearest you.

4 - Repeat Steps **2** and **3**, passing the thread through the spring coils from left to right, and winding it around the warp pegs at each end.

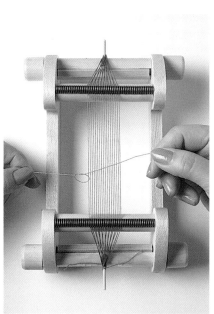

7 - Tie a weft thread to the leftmost warp thread.

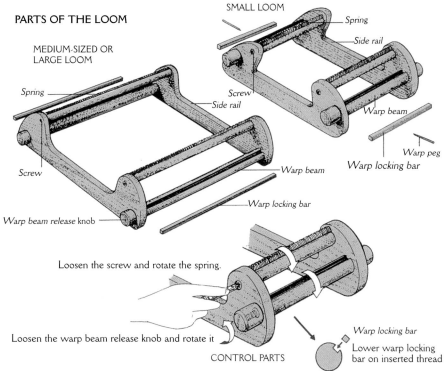

PARTS OF THE LOOM

SMALL LOOM

Spring

Side rail

Screw

Warp beam

Warp peg

Warp locking bar

MEDIUM-SIZED OR LARGE LOOM

Spring

Side rail

Screw

Warp beam

Warp locking bar

Warp beam release knob

Loosen the screw and rotate the spring.

Loosen the warp beam release knob and rotate it

CONTROL PARTS

Warp locking bar

Lower warp locking bar on inserted thread

WEAVING A SIMPLE PENDANT
(pictured on Page 18)

As you weave this pendant, you will learn the basics of beadweaving. You will also learn how to increase and decrease beads, and how to hide the warp threads.

Finished size . . . . .2.7 cm L x 4.3 cm W
Tools . . . . .Small loom; needle (small)
Thread . . . . .Gray
Additional supplies   Chain, bail, bead
                          cap, bead tip, jump ring
Number of warp threads (Method B). 18
Horizontal x vertical rows . . . . .17 x 25

BASIC WEAVING PROCEDURE

The weaving procedure remains the same, whether you use warping method A or B.

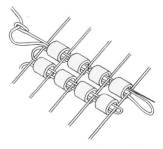

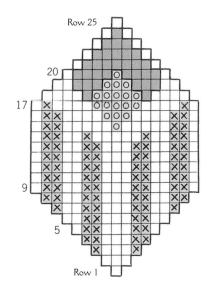

BEADS
☐ = Gray (21) . . . . .2 g
▨ = Rhodium (36) . . . . . . .1 g
◎ = Green (27C) . . . . .1 g
☒ = Gray (26) . . . . .1 g

1 - WARPING THE LOOM AND WEAVING ••

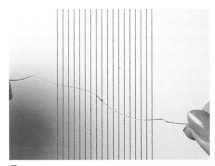

1 - Using Method B, string 18 warp threads on a small loom. Tie a weft thread onto the ninth warp thread from the left.

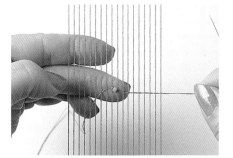

2 - String one bead onto the weft thread. Place a finger under the warp threads, and push the bead up between warp threads at the center.

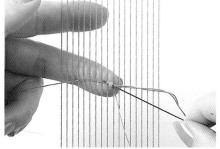

3 - Thread a beading needle with the weft thread. Insert the eye end of the needle into the hole in the bead from the right, and bring the needle out on top of the warp threads.

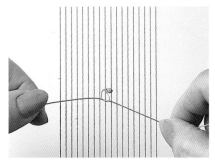

4 - Remove needle; tie the bead onto the thread where you began weaving. You have woven Row 1.

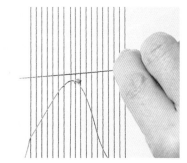

5 - Now, weave Row 2. Pass the weft thread over the warp thread to the upper left of the first bead, and then under it.

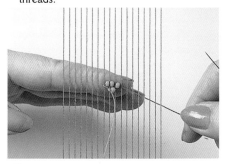

6 - Pass the needle through three beads; position each of them between warp threads with your fingers, pushing up from below.

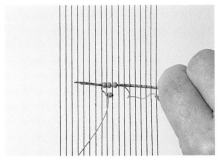

7 - Slide the eye end of the needle through the beads so that the needle passes over the warp threads.

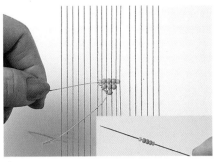

8 - Repeating **5** through **7**, slide the needle through the third row of beads.

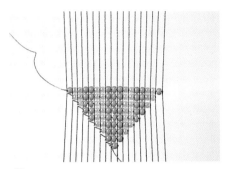

9 - Increasing one bead on each side in each row, weave up to Row 9, following the chart.

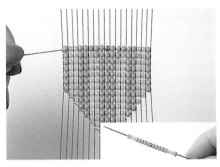

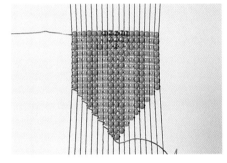

10 - Weave five rows without increasing or decreasing. Starting with Row 15, begin the center pattern. You have now completed 17 rows.

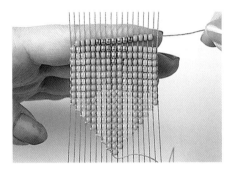

11 - Begin decreasing at Row 18. Slide needle through beads and position beads between warp threads, decreasing one bead at each side.

● **ATTACHING WEFT THREAD IN THE MIDDLE OF A PIECE**

Insert the new thread between beads already woven, and tie it on as shown below.

WEAVER'S KNOT

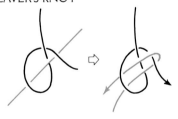

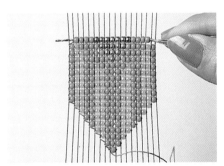

12 - Skipping warp threads at left and right edges, pass needle through beads and under warp threads at the left side.

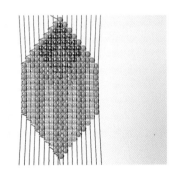

13 - Weave up to Row 25, decreasing one bead at each side.

2 - HIDING THE WEFT AND WARP THREADS ···

1 - Hide the weft thread by threading it onto a needle, winding it around the warp thread, and pulling it tight. Repeat.

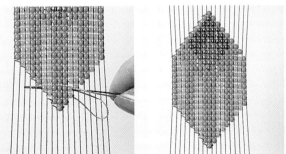

2 - Pass the needle through three or four rows of beads; cut thread at the edge of a bead. Hide the first weft thread in the same way.

HIDING THE WEFT THREADS

3 - Loosen warp beam release knob, raise warp beam, and remove warp threads from warp peg. Repeat process at the other end of the loom.

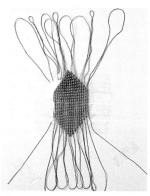

4 - Tape both warp thread ends to the board.

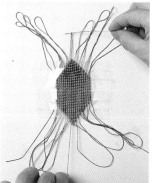

5 - Divide warp threads in half at center of piece. Hide threads, starting with leftmost warp thread. Insert needle in loop at top center of piece; pull that thread from bottom of piece until top thread is about the same length as the needle. Pull on a loop near the bottom center. Repeat with the loop near bottom center, pulling toward the top.

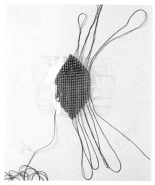

6 - Repeat (5) for entire left side of piece.

7 - Hide threads on right half of piece, alternating between top and bottom. Cut warp thread, leaving 20 cm.

8 - Insert needle threaded with remaining warp thread into Row 9, pull it out at the center, and cut.

9 - Hide weft threads, running them through piece 1-1.5 cm. Pull tight.

10 - Slide needle through the beads to the side. Bring needle out one bead short of the edge.

11 - Cut thread at the edge of a bead. Hide the warp thread on the left in the same way.

3 - ATTACHING FINDINGS ••

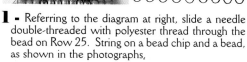

Use double polyester thread (#60)

Run weft thread through piece as shown

2 - Insert a bead into the bead tip, tie thread around it twice, and cut at the edge. Apply glue to the knot.

3 - Close the bead tip with pliers.

Bail — Jump Ring

1 - Referring to the diagram at right, slide a needle double-threaded with polyester thread through the bead on Row 25. String on a bead chip and a bead, as shown in the photographs,

4 - Attach jump ring to opening in bead tip. Attach bail and then the chain.

INCREASING AND DECREASING

So that the weft thread does not show

This method permits you to increase or decrease two or more beads without the weft threads showing. However, the weft threads on the right side will remain visible, so it is used only on the left side. When you are adding fringe or edging in an increase or decrease, you don't need to hide the weft thread.

● DECREASING

1 - Catch one warp thread at left edge, from the left, wind thread on the needle around it. In preceding row, pass needle through number of beads to be decreased.

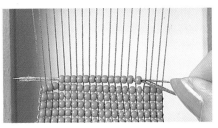

2 - Bring weft thread under warp thread, and pick up the (smaller) number of beads for the next row. Push them up between the warp threads with your fingers.

3 - Insert needle from underneath warp threads where decrease is to be made, pass it through in the opposite direction, and bring it out under warp threads where decrease is to be made on other side. Continue decreasing, following diagram, until three beads remain.

● INCREASING

1 - Pick up the number of beads that are to be increased, and pass needle under warp threads. Place beads between warp threads to left of previous row.

2 - Pass needle through the two beads increased in **1**. Again, pick up number of beads to be increased, and pass needle under warp threads. Place beads between warp threads.

3 - Pass needle through the increased beads, returning to the left side. Pick up the number of beads to be increased at the left side of next row, and place them between the warp threads. Continue increasing in this manner.

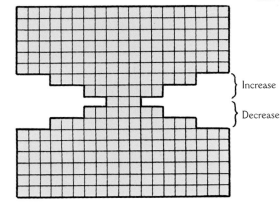

} Increase

} Decrease

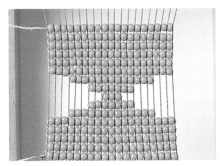

4 - Increases and decreases at left and right have been made. Notice that the weft threads do not carry over to the edges.

The way threads are hidden differs according to the warping method (A or B) that you use. See Page 42 for the procedure to follow when using Method B.

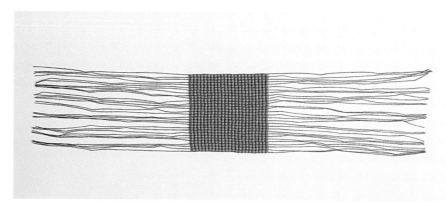

1 - When you have finished weaving, cut warp threads at both ends, and remove them from the loom. Leave an excess of 15 cm at each side.

2 - Leave warp threads at each edge as they are for the time being. Thread a needle with one of the warp threads and pick up weft threads, one at a time, running them through the piece, 3-4 cm as shown, starting on Row 2.

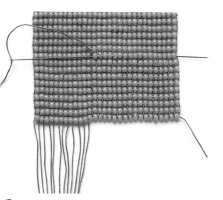

3 - Pull the needle through the threads, and slide it through the beads to the side. Bring it out at the edge, and cut the thread next to the last bead.

4 - Now, hide the warp threads at the edges. Insert the needle at the edge, pass it through about 3 cm of beads, and pull it through.

● WHEN YOU ARE ATTACHING A LINING OR BACKING

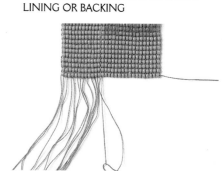

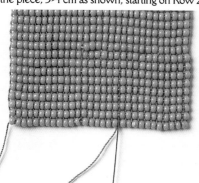

5 - Run the weft threads through the piece, one at a time, for 3 - 4 cm, starting on the second row, for 3 - 4 cm, and pull the needle through.

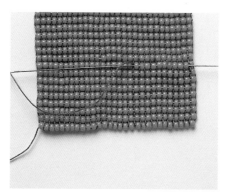

6 - Pass needle through beads to the side, bringing it out to the left of the last bead. Cut remaining warp thread at edge of the bead. Hide thread on other side in the same way.

When you are attaching a backing or lining, run the weft threads through the piece, one at a time, for about 5 cm, starting with Row 2. Cut thread, leaving an excess of 1.5 cm.

MAKING A MINIATURE PURSE BROOCH

(Pictured on Page 24)

This is a new method of weaving used to create a pattern of horizontal stripes. Here, the number of warp threads exactly matches the number of beads.

Finished Size . . . . . . .3.8 cm W x 3.8 cm L
Tools . . . . . . .Small loom, needle (medium)
Thread . . . . .Gray
Supplies . . . . .Silver ribbon-shaped pin
jump ring & bead tip
Warping method A . . . . .26 threads
Horizontal x Vertical rows . . . . . . .26 x 31

☐ =(a) Pink (422)...7 g   ☐ =(b) Silver (36C)...7 g

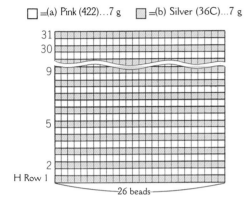

1 - String the specified number of (b) beads on the warp threads. Arrange beads neatly. Use Warping Method B, place the threads between spring coils.

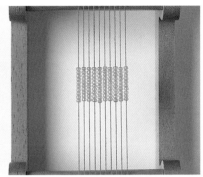

2 - Weave one row of (a) beads.

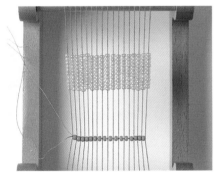

3 - Bring a row of the (b) beads on warp threads down, so they lie directly above row of (a) beads. Pass needle through (b) bead at left edge.

4 - Weave one row of (a) beads.

5 - Repeat (3) and (4) for the specified number of rows.

6 - Remove the piece from the loom, and hide threads, using Method B.

8 rows

Thread a needle with a warp thread, and sew sides together.

11 rows

Fold

Bottom (1 row of beads)

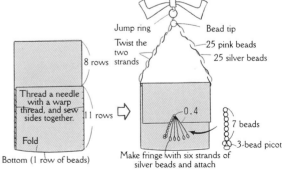

Ribbon pin

Jump ring

Twist the two strands

Bead tip

25 pink beads

25 silver beads

0.4

7 beads

3-bead picot

Make fringe with six strands of silver beads and attach

7 - Finish the brooch.

45

MAKING A BROOCH
(pictured on Page 14)

In this project, you will weave a piece with a pattern and twisted strips at the center, and learn how to make fringe.

Finished Dimensions . . . . .3.5 cm W x 7 cm L
Tools . . . . .Small loom, needle (small)
Thread . . . . .Gray
Supplies . . . . . .Flush perforated pin back (3 cm)
Warping method A . . . . . . .60 cm x 24 threads
Horizontal x Vertical rows . . . . .28 x 23

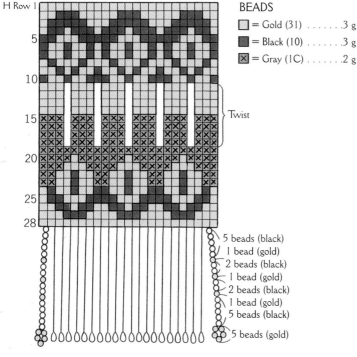

H Row 1

5

10

15

20

25

28

Twist

BEADS

☐ = Gold (31) . . . . . . .3 g
■ = Black (10) . . . . . . .3 g
☒ = Gray (1C) . . . . . .2 g

5 beads (black)
1 bead (gold)
2 beads (black)
1 bead (gold)
2 beads (black)
1 bead (gold)
5 beads (black)
5 beads (gold)

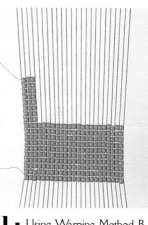

1 - Using Warping Method B, string 24 warp threads. Weave straight, following pattern for 10 rows. Starting with Row 11, weave eight rows of three beads.

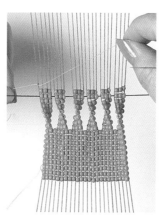

5 - Replace the warp threads on the loom; tie a weft thread to the warp thread at the left edge with a weaver's knot.

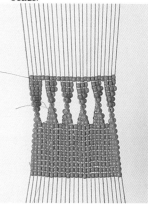

6 - Weave one row with the weft thread from **5**.

10 - Pull the needle through, leaving about 10 cm excess. String the beads for the fringe on the thread.

11 - Pass the needle through all beads, except those for the picot. Insert needle in the second bead from the left edge, and pull the thread through. You have completed one strand of the fringe.

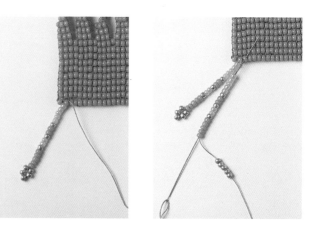

12 - String beads for next strand. Pass needle through all beads, except those for picot. Insert needle into third bead from left edge; pull thread through. Repeat process for the remaining strands.

46

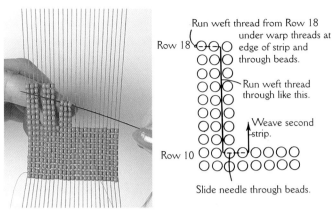

Row 18 ○○○ Run weft thread from Row 18
under warp threads at
edge of strip and
through beads.

Run weft thread
through like this.

Weave second
strip.

Row 10 ○○○○○
Slide needle through beads.

2 - Following diagram at right, bring the weft thread to the location where the next center strip will be woven, and begin weaving.

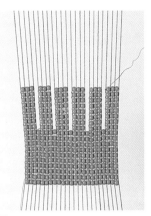

3 - Weave all six strips in the same way. Wind the weft thread twice around the fourth bead from right; run it back through the beads and cut.

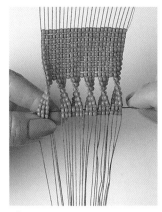

4 - Remove warp threads from top of loom. Twist each strip once. Secure strips by running the needle through the second row of beads from the bottom.

7 - Weave straight, following the pattern, through Row 28.

8 - Remove piece from loom; cut warp threads so that 15 cm remain. See Page 44 for instructions on hiding threads.

9 - To attach fringe, thread needle, insert it into the second bead from right edge, and bring it out to the left of second bead from left edge.

13 - You have completed the 22-strand fringe.

Wrong Side

14 - Attach a flush perforated pin back. Place pin back on beadwork. Thread a needle with double thread. Pass it through two beads, then into a hole in pin back; repeat.

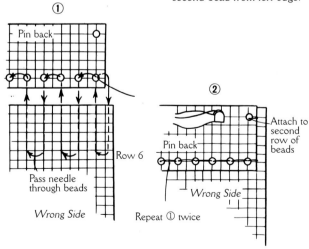

①

Pin back

Row 6

Pass needle through beads

Wrong Side

②

Pin back

Attach to second row of beads

Wrong Side

Repeat ① twice

HAND-WOVEN NECKLACE AND BRACELET

These pieces are made using only a needle and thread.

NECKLACE WITH MINIATURE FLOWERS

● INSTRUCTIONS

1 Thread needle with 80 cm of polyester thread. String 2 silver beads, 2 pink beads, and 1 green bead on thread (up to 5 on chart at right).
2 Following chart at right, pass the needle through 3, 6, and 1.
3 Now, pass the needle through 7 and 6.
4 Pass the needle through 8 and 5.
5 Pass the needle through 9 and 8.
6 Pass the needle through 10 and 7.
7 Pass the needle through 11 and 10.
8 Pass the needle through 12 and 9.
9 Pass the needle through 13, 14, and 15, and then through 4, 3, 8, and 9. You have completed one pattern.
10 Now, pass the needle through 16 and 12. Continue working, following the chart, until the piece measures 100 cm.

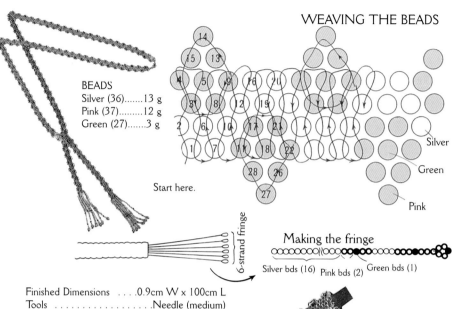

WEAVING THE BEADS

BEADS
Silver (36).......13 g
Pink (37).........12 g
Green (27).......3 g

Start here.

Silver

Green

Pink

6-strand fringe

Making the fringe

Silver bds (16) Pink bds (2) Green bds (1)

Finished Dimensions . . . .0.9cm W x 100cm L
Tools . . . . .Needle (medium)
Thread . . . . .Gray

BRACELET WITH MINIATURE FLOWERS (B)

Finished Dimensions .1.2 cm W x 17.5 cm L
Tools . . . . .Needle (medium)
Thread . . . . .Gray
Supplies . . . . . . .Bracelet clasp, bead tips (2)
jump rings (2)

BEADS
Silver (36)..........4 g
Pink (37)............3 g
Green (27)........1 g

BEADS
Gold (31)..............7 g
Green (27)............1 g

Finished Dimensions . . . . . . .5cm W x 17cm L
Tools . . . . .Needle (medium)
Thread . . . . .Gray
Supplies . . . . .Three-strand bracelet clasp

● INSTRUCTIONS

Attach three-strand clasp to both ends of the bracelet.

WEAVING THE BEADS

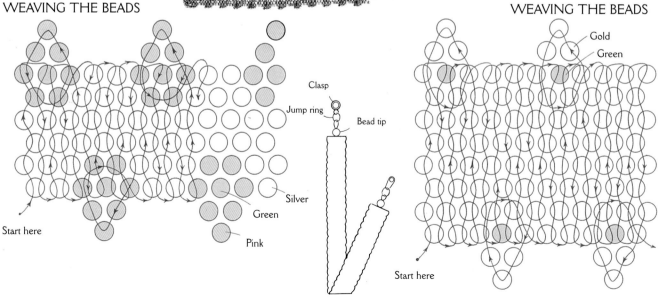

Start here

Silver

Green

Pink

Clasp

Jump ring

Bead tip

WEAVING THE BEADS

Gold

Green

Start here

OVAL BROOCH (A)

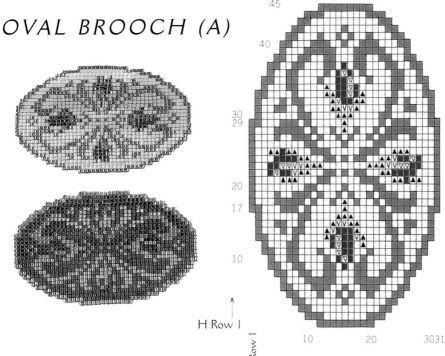

H Row 1

V Row 1

Finished Dimensions . . .5 cm W x 7.5 cm L
Tools . . . . . . .Small loom, needle (medium)
Thread . . . . .Gray [Black]
Supplies . . . . . . .Flush perforated pin back
Warping method A . . . .60 cm x 32 threads
Horizontal x Vertical rows . . . . . . .45 x 31

● INSTRUCTIONS

Make increases at left and right from Row 1 through Row 17. At Row 30, begin decreasing. Hide threads and attach pin back (see Page 47).

Text in brackets [ ] refers only to the black pin. Otherwise, the procedure is the same as for the white pin.

BEADS

□ = Cream (203)/Black [10]	5 g
▒ = Gold (21)	4 g
◼ = Pink (56)/Red [62]	1 g
▽ = Pink (72)/Orange [54]	1 g
▲ = Green (27C)/Green (327)	1 g
∨ = Lime (60)	1 g

TYROLEAN RIBBON BROOCH

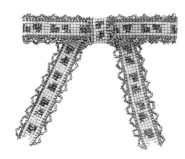

Finished Dimensions .7.5cm W x 8.5cm L
Tools . . . . . . .Small loom, needle (small)
Thread . . . . .Gray [Black]
Supplies . . . . .Pin back (small)
Warping method A . . . .60 cm x 8 threads
Horizontal x Vertical rows: A . . . .96 x 7
                                            B . . . .44 x 7
                                            C . . . .20 x 7

● INSTRUCTIONS

Weave one each of A and C, weave two of B; hide threads. Attach 5-bead loops at the edges of each piece. Sew ends of A together at center back. Attach the two B pieces at both sides of the seam, so that they form a "V." Wrap C around the center of A, and attach. Attach pin back.

A (Half of finished piece)   B (Make two)   C   FORMING THE RIBBON

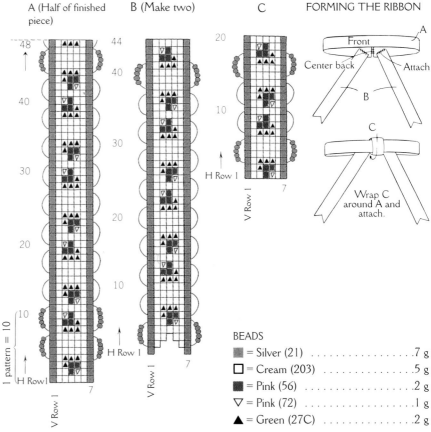

1 pattern = 10

H Row 1

V Row 1

BEADS

▒ = Silver (21)	. . . .	.7 g
□ = Cream (203)	. . . .	.5 g
◼ = Pink (56)	. . . .	.2 g
▽ = Pink (72)	. . . .	.1 g
▲ = Green (27C)	. . . .	.2 g

49

SQUARE-CUT BROOCH

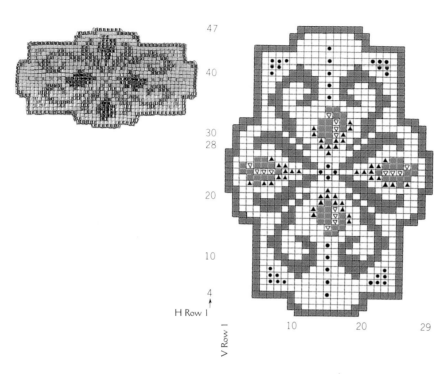

Finished Dimensionms .5 cm W x 8 cm L
Tools . . . . .Small loom, needle (medium)
Thread . . . . .Gray
Supplies .Flush perforated pin back (6 cm)
Warping method A . . .60 cm x 30 threads
Horizontal x Vertical rows . . . . . .47 x 29

● INSTRUCTIONS

Make increases at left and right from Row 1
through Row 21. Begin decreasing on Row
28. Hide threads; attach pin back (see Page
47).

BEADS

☐ = Cream (203) . . . . .5 g
▦ = Silver (21) . . . . .4 g
▽ = Pink (72) . . . . .1 g
▨ = Pink (56) . . . . .1 g
▲ = Green (27C) . . . . .1 g
● = Silver (36C) . . . . .1 g

OVAL BROOCH - B

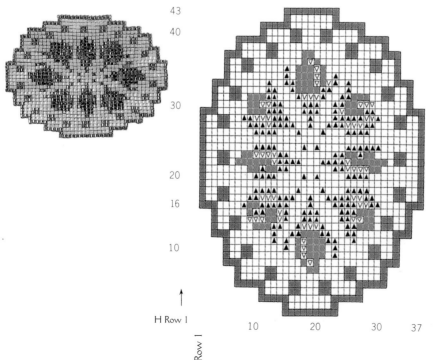

Finished Dimensions 5.5 cm W x 7 cm L
Tools . . . . .Small loom, needle (medium)
Thread . . . . .Gray
Supplies
        Flush perforated pin back (4.5 cm)
Warping method A   . .60cm x 38 threads
Horizontal x Vertical rows . . . . .43 x 37

● INSTRUCTIONS

Make increases at left and right from Row 1
through Row 16. Begin decreasing on Row
30. Hide threads; attach pin back (see Page
47).

BEADS

☐ = Cream (203) . . . . .5 g
▨ = Silver (21) . . . . .2 g
▲ = Green (27C) . . . . .2 g
▨ = Pink (56) . . . . .2 g
▽ = Pink (72) . . . . .1 g
∨ = Lime (60) . . . . .1 g

FLOWERED HAT BROOCH

Finished measurements . .7.5 cm W x 8 cm L
Tools . . . . . . .Small loom, needle (medium)
Thread . . . . .Beige
Supplies . . . .Flush perforated pin back (3 cm)
Warping method A   A . .60 cm x 52 threads
                   B . . .60 cm x 6 threads
Horizontal x Vertical rows   A . . . . .47 x 51
                             B . . . . . .76 x 5

● INSTRUCTIONS

Weave A; hide threads. In the center circle, make picots, working toward the middle of the circle. Fill the space with picots, making 3-bead picots in the first round and 5-bead picots in the second round and thereafter. Weave B; hide threads. Fold B in half diagonally, and attach to the bottom of the center of A. Attach pin back (see Page 47).

BEADS

☐ = Trans (141) .13 g   ▽ = Pink (72) . . . .1 g
▨ = Wh (201) . . .6 g   ▩ = Pink (56) . . . .1 g
▲ = Grn (27C) . . .1 g

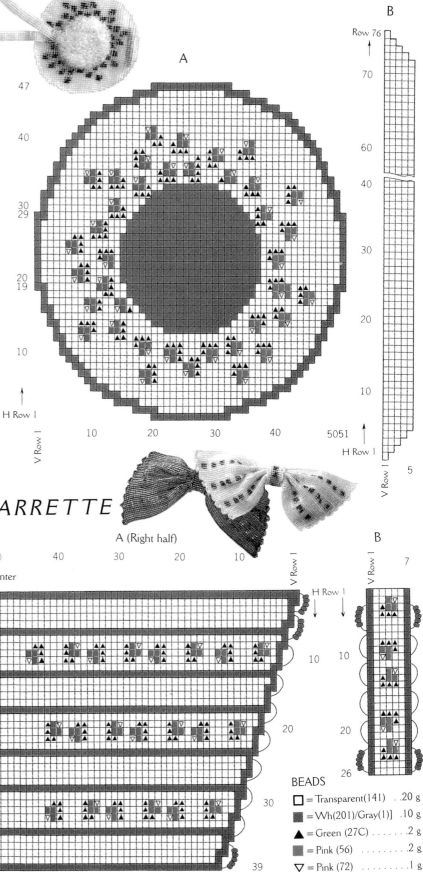

DRAPED RIBBON BARRETTE

Finished measurements .7 cm W x 13 cm L
Tools Medium-sized loom, needle (medium)
Thread . . . . .Beige [Black]
Supplies . . . . .Barrette back (6 cm)
Warping method A   A 90 cm x 101 threads
                   B   8 threads
Horizontal x Vertical rows A . . . .39 x 100
                            B . . . . . .26 x 7

● INSTRUCTIONS

The chart shows half of A. Weave 100 beads on the first two rows. Begin decreasing at left and right on Row 3. Hide threads. Weave B; hide threads. Attach 5-bead loops to edges of A and B. Gather A at the center, wrap B around it, and attach. Attach barrette back.

Text in brackets [ ] refers to the black barrette. Otherwise, the procedure is the same as for the white barrette.

BEADS

☐ = Transparent(141) . .20 g
▨ = Wh(201)/Gray(1)] .10 g
▲ = Green (27C) . . . . . . .2 g
▩ = Pink (56) . . . . .2 g
▽ = Pink (72) . . . . .1 g

TREBLE CLEF BROOCH

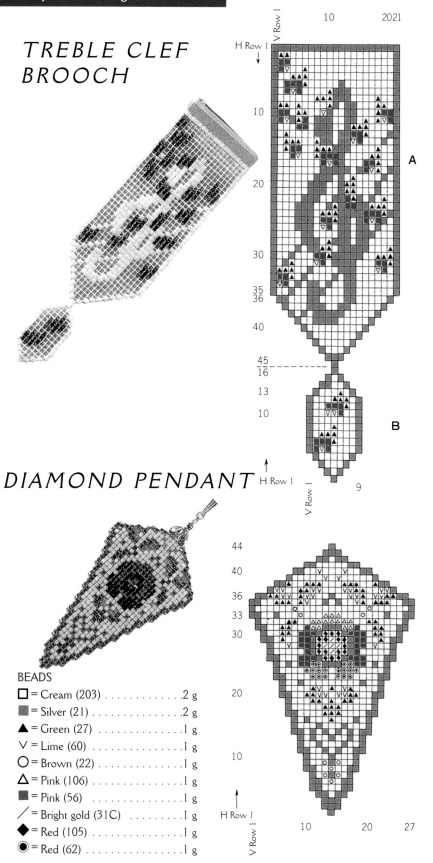

DIAMOND PENDANT

Finished Dimensions .3 cm W x 10.5 cm L
Tools . .Medium-sized loom, needle (small)
Thread . . . . .Beige
Supplies . . . . . .Perforated pin back (3 cm)
Warping method B   A . . . . .22 threads
                       B . . . . .10 threads
Horizontal x Vertical rows: A   45 x 21
                                  B . . . .19 x 9

● INSTRUCTIONS

Weave A and B separately. For A, weave Rows 1 through 35. Begin decreasing at left and right on Row 36. Continue decreasing until Row 45. Hide threads. Weave B, following instructions for pendant on Page 40. Hide threads. Join the two pieces using separate thread; attach pin back (see Page 47).

BEADS

▨ = White (201)	. . . .	.3 g
☐ = Transparent (141)	. . . .	.2 g
▲ = Green (27C)	. . . .	.1 g
◼ = Pink (56)	. . . .	.1 g
▽ = Pink (72)	. . . .	.1 g

BEADS

☐ = Cream (203)	. . . .	.2 g
▨ = Silver (21)	. . . .	.2 g
▲ = Green (27)	. . . .	.1 g
∨ = Lime (60)	. . . .	.1 g
○ = Brown (22)	. . . .	.1 g
△ = Pink (106)	. . . .	.1 g
◼ = Pink (56)	. . . .	.1 g
╱ = Bright gold (31C)	. . . .	.1 g
◆ = Red (105)	. . . .	.1 g
◉ = Red (62)	. . . .	.1 g

Finished Dimensions . .4 cm W x 7 cm L
Tools . . . . . .Small loom, needle (medium)
Thread . . . . .Gray
Supplies . . . . .Chain, bail, bead cap,
                          bead tip, jump ring
Warping method B . . . . .28 threads
Horizontal x Vertical rows . . . . . .44 x 27

● INSTRUCTIONS

From Row 1 through Row 33, make increases at left and right. Begin decreasing at Row 36. Hide threads. Attach findings to center of piece (see Page 42).

ROUND PENDANT

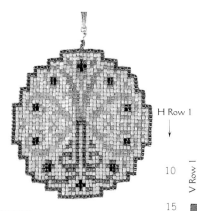

H Row 1

Finished Dimensions . . . .6 cm W x 6.5 cm L
Tools . . . . .Small loom, needle (medium)
Thread . . . . .Gray [Black]
Supplies . . . . .Chain, bail, bead cap,
bead tip, jump ring, [spring ring,
bail, bead cap, chain tag;
bead tips, jump rings (three each)]
Warping method A . . . . .60 cm x 42 threads
Horizontal x Vertical rows . . . . .39 x 41

● INSTRUCTIONS

Weave Rows 1 through 15, making increases on the left and right. Start decreasing on Row 26. Hide threads. Attach findings to the center of Row 39 (see Page 42). [For the chain, thread approximately 65 cm of beads on three 90-cm strands of thread, and braid them rather tightly.]

BEADS

□ = Cream (203)/Black [10] .5 g
▲ = Green (238) . . . . .3 g
● = Green (327) . . . . .1 g
▨ = Silver (21)/Gray [1] . . . .2 g
◼ = Pink (56) . . . . .1 g
○ = Red (105) . . . . .1 g
∨ = Lime (60) . . . . .1 g

You will also need 10 g of Gray [21] for the chain.

Text in brackets [ ] refers to the black pendant. Otherwise, the procedure is the same as for the white pendant.

ATTACHING THE FINDINGS
[BLACK PENDANT]

FRONT   BACK

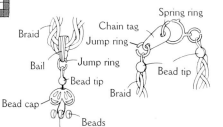

Braid
Chain tag
Spring ring
Jump ring
Jump ring
Bail
Bead tip
Jump ring
Bead tip
Bead cap
Braid
Center bead
Beads

HAIRBAND

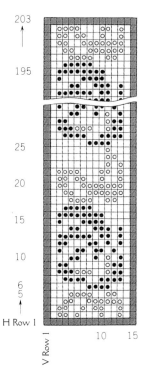

Finished Dimensions . . .2.2 cm W x 33 cm L
Tools . . . . .Small loom, needle (medium)
Thread . . . . .Black
Supplies . . . . . . .Gray hairband (2.5 cm W)
Warping method A . . . . . .60 cm x 16 threads
Horizontal x Vertical rows . . . . .203 x 15

● INSTRUCTIONS

Weave Rows 1 through 5. Rows 6 through Row 25 will form one complete pattern; repeat 10 times. Weave additional rows if the length of the piece does not match that of the hairband. Hide threads; sew piece to hairband.

BEADS

□ = Transparent (141) . . . . .10 g
● = Black (10C) . . . . .6 g
▨ = Silver (21) . . . . .4 g
○ = Gray (1) . . . . .4 g

RIBBON BARRETTE

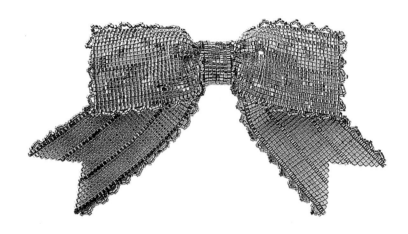

Finished Dimensions   . . .8 cm W x 14 cm L
Tools   . . . . . . .Small loom, needle (medium)
Thread . . . . .Black
Supplies . . . . .Barrette back (6 cm)
Warping method A   A 80 cm x 24 threads
            B   B . . . . .8 threads
            A   C 80 cm x 22 threads
Horizontal x vertical rows   A . . . . .68 x 23
                         B . . . . . .26 x 7
                         C . . . .108 x 21

● INSTRUCTIONS

Weave A, B, and C; hide threads. Attach 5-bead picots to the edges of each piece. Place A on top of C, gather center and baste. Sew barrette back onto wrong side of piece. Wrap B around center and attach.

A

B

C

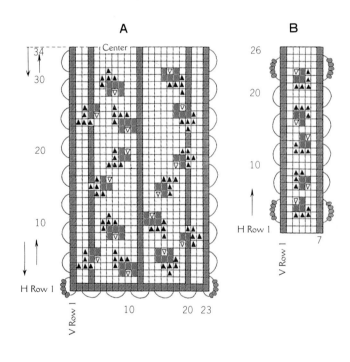

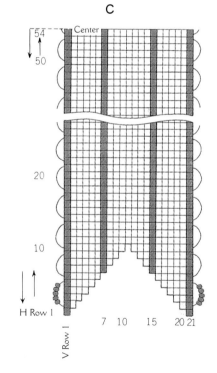

BEADS
□ = Transparent (141) . . . . .22 g
▦ = Gray (1) . . . . .8 g
▲ = Green (27C) . . . . .2 g
▨ = Pink (56) . . . . .2 g
▽ = Pink (72) . . . . .1 g

54

RUCHED HAIR ORNAMENT

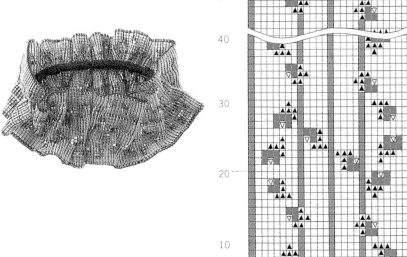

Finished Dimensions	.10cm x 14cm circle
Tools	Small loom, needle (small)
Thread	Black
Supplies	Black 5-mm-thick elastic (16 cm)
Warping method A	.90 cm x 28 threads
Horizontal x Vertical rows	.280 x 27

● INSTRUCTIONS

Weave Rows 1 through 20 to form one pattern; repeat 14 times. Join the piece to form a circle; hide threads. Join elastic band to form a circle. Gather woven piece

BEADS

☐ = Transparent (141) . . . . .34 g
▨ = Gray (1) . . . . .10 g
▲ = Green (27C) . . . . .7 g
▨ = Pink (56) . . . . .4 g
▽ = Pink (72) . . . . .2 g

SQUARE BROOCH

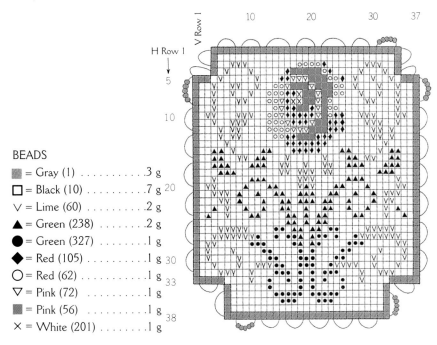

Finished Dimensions	.6 cm W x 7 cm L
Tools	Small loom, needle (medium)
Thread	Gray
Supplies	Flush perforated pin back (4.5 cm)
Warping method B	.38 threads
Horizontal x Vertical rows	.38 x 37

● INSTRUCTIONS

Weave Rows 1 through 4. Begin increasing at left and right in Row 5. Weave up to Row 33. Begin decreasing at left and right in Row 34. End with Row 38. Hide threads. Attach 5-bead picots to edges. Attach pin back at Row 3 (see Page 47).

BEADS

▨ = Gray (1) . . . . .3 g
☐ = Black (10) . . . . .7 g
∨ = Lime (60) . . . . .2 g
▲ = Green (238) . . . . . . .2 g
● = Green (327) . . . . . . .1 g
◆ = Red (105) . . . . .1 g
○ = Red (62) . . . . .1 g
▽ = Pink (72) . . . . .1 g
▨ = Pink (56) . . . . .1 g
✕ = White (201) . . . . . . .1 g

SMALL TRIANGULAR BAG

Finished Dimensions .12.5 cm W x 18 cm L
Tools .Medium-sized loom, needle (large set)
Thread . . . . .Black
Supplies . . . . .Black fabric for lining
    (15 cm x 40 cm), two lengths of steel
    .boning (1 cm W x 11 cm L)
Warping method A A .90 cm x 86 threads
         B B . . . . .8 threads
         A C .150 cm x 8 threads
Horizontal x Vertical rows
        A . .85 x 317 (105 rows)
        B . . . . .42 x 7
        C . . . . .720 x 7

● INSTRUCTIONS

Weave A (the front, back, and flap of the bag) in one piece (see instructions at right). First, weave the front, decreasing through Row 106. Next, weave the back, following the pattern backwards from Row 105 to Row 1. Then, weave the flap by decreasing 6 beads at both left and right, leaving 73 beads. Weave, following the chart, until you have completed 106 rows. When you pull the warp threads tight where the increases or decreases on both sides were made, the bag will assume its proper shape. Attach 5-bead loops to both sides of the flap.

Now, weave the strap. Rows 1 through 60 will form one pattern (approximately 10 cm); repeat these rows five times (the flower design should appear five times). Then, weave 60 rows of black beads until you have completed the left side of the strap (360 rows or about 60 cm). Then work backwards from Rows 360 through 1, for a total of 720 rows (about 120 cm). Hide threads, and finish bag, following instructions on this page.

WEAVING PROCEDURE

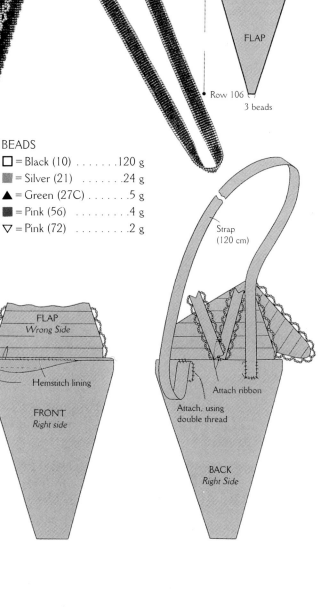

Row 1 — 85 beads — Opening
FRONT (First piece)
15 bds
Row 106
Row 105
BACK (Second piece)
Row 1 — 85 beads
Row 1 — 73 beads
FLAP
Row 106 — 3 beads

BEADS

□ = Black (10) . . . . . . .120 g
▨ = Silver (21) . . . . . . .24 g
▲ = Green (27C) . . . . . . .5 g
▪ = Pink (56) . . . . .4 g
▽ = Pink (72) . . . . .2 g

MAKING THE LINING

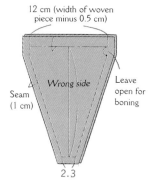

12 cm (width of woven piece minus 0.5 cm)
Wrong side
Seam (1 cm)
Leave open for boning
2.3

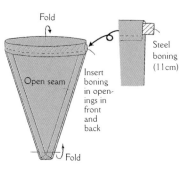

Fold
Open seam
Insert boning in openings in front and back
Steel boning (11cm)
Fold

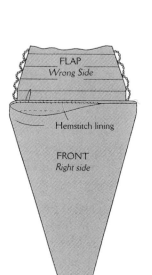

FLAP
Wrong Side
Hemstitch lining
FRONT
Right side

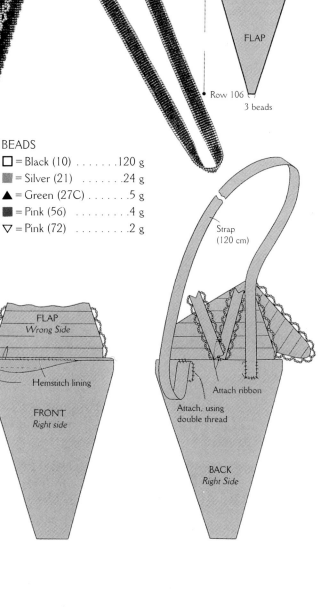

Strap (120 cm)
Attach ribbon
Attach, using double thread
BACK
Right Side

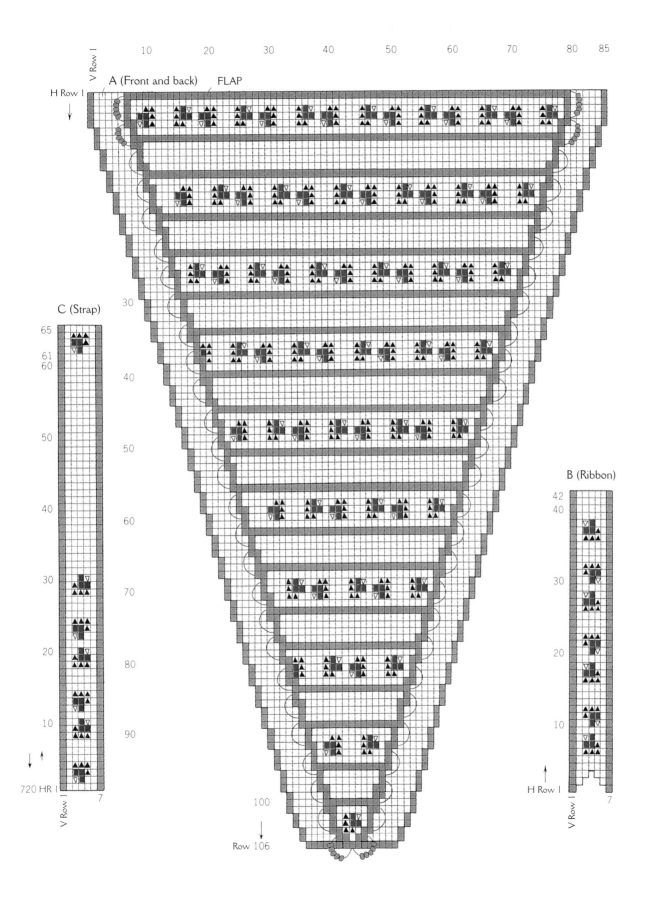

PETIT-POINT CASE

Finished Dim . . . . .9.5cm W x 17.5cm L
Tools . .Medium-sized loom, needle (large)
Thread . . . . .Black
Supplies . . . . .Black fabric for lining
        (12.5 cm x 42 cm), two lengths
        of steel boning (1 cm W x 8 cm L)
Warping method A . . .90 cm x 65 threads
Horizontal x Vertical rows . . . . .213 x 64

● INSTRUCTIONS

Start weaving at Row 1. Starting with Row 90, form the curved bottom of the case by decreasing at left and right through Row 107. Starting with Row 106, weave the bottom of the other side of the case, increasing at left and right. Weave back to Row 1. Following the instructions on this page, cut warp threads, leaving 15 cm. Fold the piece in half, pull the threads, and hide them. Make the lining, following the instructions below.

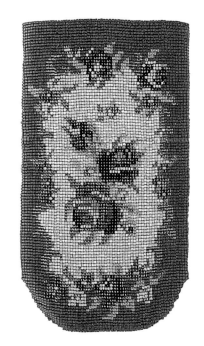

FINISHING INSTRUCTIONS

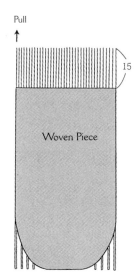

Pull
15
Woven Piece

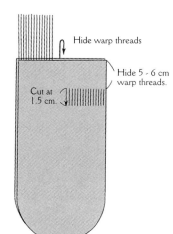

Hide warp threads
Hide 5 - 6 cm warp threads.
Cut at 1.5 cm.

Thread warp and weft threads at edges onto a needle; sew sides together.

MAKING THE LINING

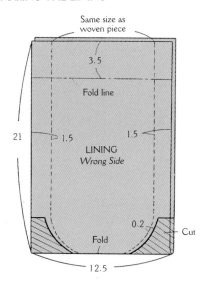

Same size as woven piece
3.5
Fold line
21
1.5
1.5
LINING
Wrong Side
0.2
Fold
Cut
12.5

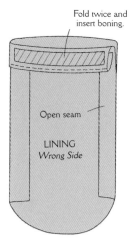

Fold twice and insert boning.
Open seam
LINING
Wrong Side

Sew lining to Row 2 of woven piece
WOVEN PIECE
Right side

BEADS

▦ = Black (310)	. .	.40 g
☐ = Cream (52)	.	.20 g
▲ = Green (27)	. .	.6 g
∨ = Lime (60)	. . .	.5 g
∧ = Topaz	. . . .	.4 g
◯ = Red (75)	. . . .	.4 g
▨ = Red (105)	. . .	.3 g
△ = Orange (67)	. .	.2 g
◎ = Purple (59)	. .	.2 g
╱ = Purple (135)	. .	.2 g
◉ = Blue (79)	. . . .	.2 g
◇ = Blue (77)	. . . . .	.1 g
▽ = Pink (70)	. . . . .	.1 g
◆ = Pink (103)	. . . .	.1 g
● = Gold (327)	. . .	.1 g
✕ = Yellow (53)	. . .	.1 g

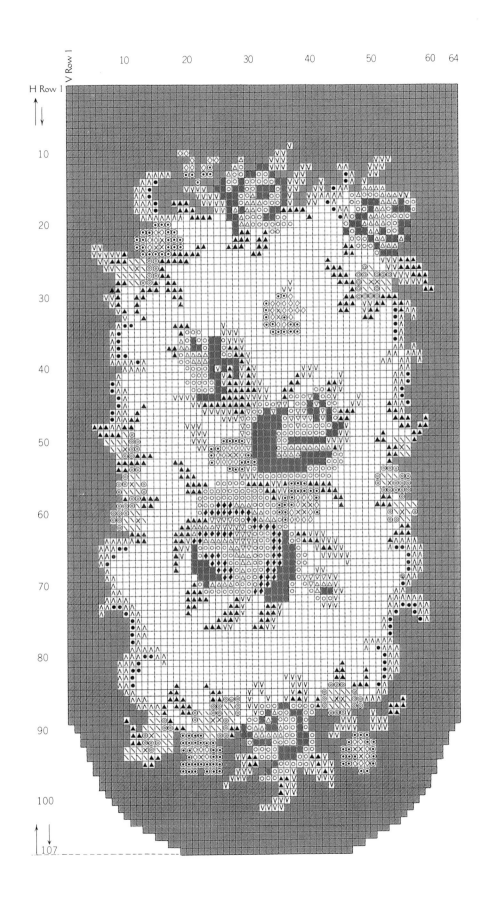

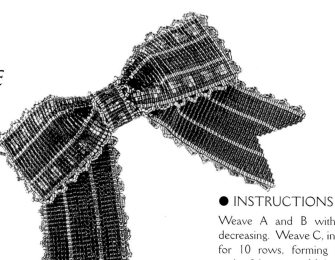

RIBBON BARRETTE

Finished Dimensions . . . .9 cm W x 11 cm L
Tools . . . . . . .Small loom, needle (medium)
Thread . . . . .Black
Supplies . . . . .Barrette back (6 cm)
Warping method A   A 60 cm x 22 threads
               B   B . . . . . . .8 threads
               A   C 80 cm x 22 threads
Horizontal x Vertical rows: A . . . . . .66 x 21
                             B . . . . . .26 x 7
                             C . . . . .108 x 21

● INSTRUCTIONS

Weave A and B without increasing or decreasing. Weave C, increasing as shown, for 10 rows, forming the arrow-shaped ends of the piece. Hide threads. Attach 5-bead picots to both edges. Place A on top of C, gather at center, and baste. Sew barrette back onto the wrong side, wrap B around center and attach.

A

B

C

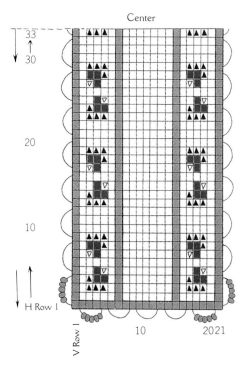

BEADS

☐ = Black (10) . . . . .20 g
▨ = Silver (21) . . . . .8 g
■ = Pink (56) . . . . .1 g
▽ = Pink (72) . . . . .1 g
▲ = Green (27C) . . . . .1 g

SHOOTING STAR EMBLEM

Finished Dimensions . .4.5cm W x 10.5cm L
Tools . . . . . . .Small loom, needle (medium)
Thread . . . . .Gray
Supplies . . . . . .Perforated pin back (4.5 cm)
Warping method A   A . . .60 cm x 32 threads
                   B . . .60 cm x 19 threads
Horizontal x Vertical rows: A . . . .45 x 31
                              B . . . .18 x 18

● INSTRUCTIONS

Weave A and B separately. For A, weave Rows 1 through 25, and then Rows 26 through 45, increasing at left and right. Hide threads. For B, weave Rows 1 through 18, increasing and decreasing as shown. Hide threads. Sew the two pieces together using a separate strand of thread. Attach pin back (see Page 47).

Text in brackets [ ] refers to the silver emblem. Otherwise, the procedure is the same as for the gold emblem.

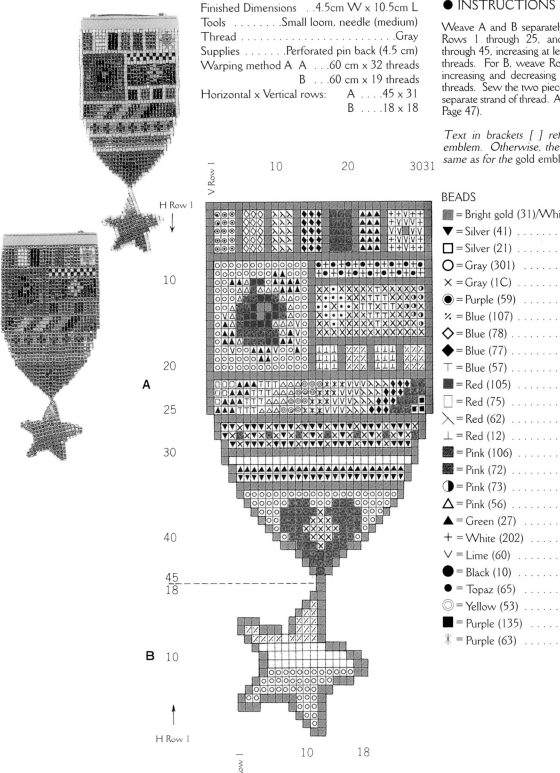

BEADS

▨ = Bright gold (31)/White [201] . .4 g
▼ = Silver (41) . . . . .2 g
☐ = Silver (21) . . . . .2 g
○ = Gray (301) . . . . .2 g
✕ = Gray (1C) . . . . .1 g
◉ = Purple (59) . . . . .1 g
✕ = Blue (107) . . . . .1 g
◇ = Blue (78) . . . . .1 g
◆ = Blue (77) . . . . .1 g
⊤ = Blue (57) . . . . .1 g
▣ = Red (105) . . . . .1 g
☐ = Red (75) . . . . .1 g
✗ = Red (62) . . . . .1 g
⊥ = Red (12) . . . . .1 g
▦ = Pink (106) . . . . .1 g
▨ = Pink (72) . . . . .1 g
◐ = Pink (73) . . . . .1 g
△ = Pink (56) . . . . .1 g
▲ = Green (27) . . . . .1 g
+ = White (202) . . . . .1 g
∨ = Lime (60) . . . . .1 g
● = Black (10) . . . . .1 g
● = Topaz (65) . . . . .1 g
◎ = Yellow (53) . . . . .1 g
■ = Purple (135) . . . . .1 g
✳ = Purple (63) . . . . .1 g

FLAG EMBLEM

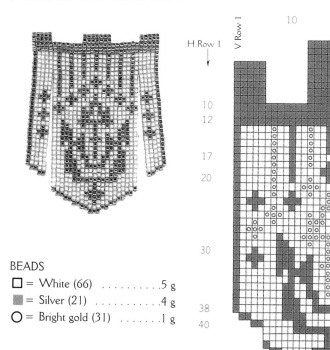

H Row 1

V Row 1   10   20   3031

10
12

17

20

30

38
40

48

BEADS

☐ = White (66) . . . . .5 g
▨ = Silver (21) . . . . .4 g
○ = Bright gold (31) . . . . . . .1 g

Finished Dimensions . . .5 cm W x 7 cm L
Tools . . . . . .Small loom, needle (medium)
Thread . . . . .Gray
Supplies . . .Arrow-shaped pin back (7 cm)
Warping method B . . . . .34 threads
Horizontal x Vertical rows: . . . . . .48 x 31

● INSTRUCTIONS

Following the chart below, warp the loom with double thread between and Ü and j and Ü. Weave _ from Row 10 through Row 17; then, starting with Row 18, weave j, Ü, and separately. Add top strips, weaving (a), (b), and then (c). Hide threads; attach pin back to top strips.

ATTACHING THE PIN BACK

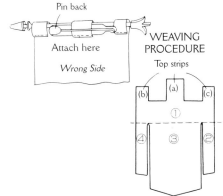

Pin back

Attach here

Wrong Side

WEAVING PROCEDURE

Top strips

(b) (a) (c)
①
④ ③ ②

SAPPHIRE EMBLEM

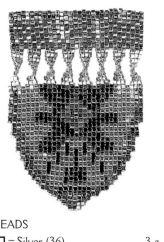

H Row 1

V Row 1   10   20   3031

8
9

16
17

24

30

40
42

BEADS

☐ = Silver (36) . . . . .3 g
▨ = Purple (29) . . . . .2 g
✕ = Dark blue (2) . . . . .2 g
○ = Bright gold (31C) . . . . . .1 g
╱ = Blue (44) . . . . .1 g
● = Gray (301) . . . . .1 g
▧ = Red (43) . . . . .1 g

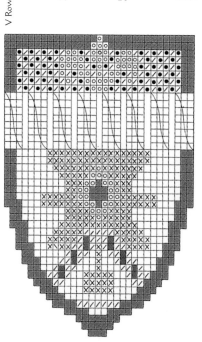

Finished Dimensions4.5 cm W x 7 cm L
Tools . . . .Small loom, needle (medium)
Thread .Gray
Supplies . . . . .Flush perforated
pin back (4.5 cm)
Warping method A .60 cm x 32 threads
Horizontal x Vertical rows . . . . .42 x 31

● INSTRUCTIONS

Weave Rows 1 through 8. Between Rows 9 and 16, make strips by weaving three beads and leaving one space open; repeat. Twist strips (see Page 46). Weave Rows 25 through 42, decreasing at left and right. Hide threads. Attach pin back to Row 2 (see Page 47).

FLOWER GARDEN EMBLEM

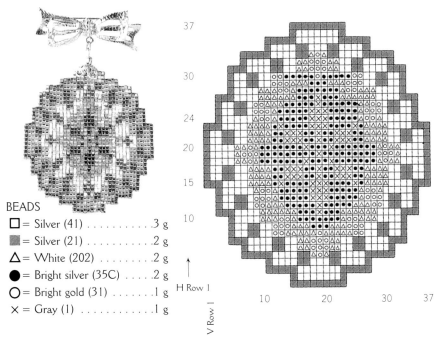

Finished Dimensions . .5.5 cm W x 6 cm L
Tools . . . . . .Small loom, needle (medium)
Thread . . . . .Gray
Supplies . . . . .Ribbon-shaped pin (4.5 cm),
bead cap, jump ring, bead tip
Warping method A . . .60 cm x 38 threads
Horizontal x Vertical rows . . . . . .37 x 37

● INSTRUCTIONS

From Rows 1 through 15, make increases at left and right to form a semicircle. Start decreasing at Row 24, and complete the circle by weaving up to Row 37. Hide threads. Attach pin back at center of Row 37.

BEADS

☐ = Silver (41) . . . . .3 g
▨ = Silver (21) . . . . .2 g
△ = White (202) . . . . .2 g
● = Bright silver (35C) . . . . .2 g
○ = Bright gold (31) . . . . . . .1 g
✕ = Gray (1) . . . . .1 g

RUBY EMBLEM

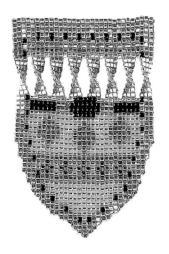

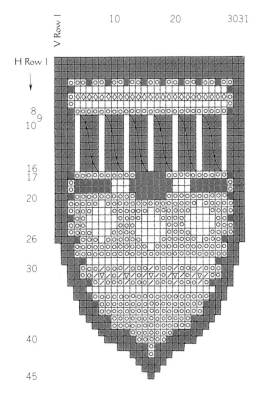

BEADS

○ = Silver (41) . . . . .4 g
▨ = Bright gold (31) . . . . . . .3 g
☐ = Silver (21) . . . . .2 g
▦ = Red (105) . . . . .1 g
◇ = Blue (44) . . . . .1 g
╱ = Gray (1) . . . . .1 g
▽ = Pink (72) . . . . .1 g

Finished Dimensions .4.5cm W x 7.5cm L
Tools . . . . . .Small loom, needle (medium)
Thread . . . . .Gray
Supplies . . . . .Flush perforated
pin back (4.5 cm)
Warping method A . . .60 cm x 32 threads
Horizontal x Vertical rows: . . . . . .45 x 31

● INSTRUCTIONS

Weave Rows 1 through 8. Between Rows 9 through 16, make strips by leaving one space and weaving three spaces (see p. 46). Begin decreasing at left and right in Row 27. Weave up to Row 45. Hide threads. Attach pin back at Row 3 (see Page 47).

SEMICIRCULAR BARRETTE

Finished Dimensions .3.8 cm W x 6 cm L
Tools . . . . .Small loom, needle (medium)
Thread . . . . .Black
Supplies . . . . .Semicircular barrette back
(4.5 cm), cardboard, black satin
brocade for lining (5 cm x 11 cm)
Warping method A . .60 cm x 25 threads
Horizontal x Vertical rows . . . . .57 x 24

● INSTRUCTIONS

In Row 1, weave 12 beads at center. Starting in Row 2, make increases at left and right until you have completed 21 rows. Starting in Row 38, make increases at left and right until you have completed 57 rows. Hide threads. Cut cardboard to the measurements specified above; attach barrette back (see instructions below).

BEADS

☐ = Black (10) . . . . .5 g
◯ = Bright gold (31) . . . . .3 g
● = Gold (22) . . . . .1 g
▨ = Gray (1) . . . . .1 g

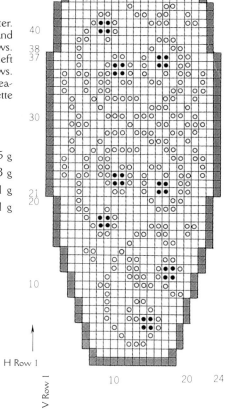

PATTERN FOR BARRETTE BACKING
(actual size)

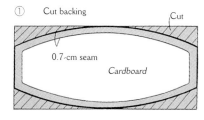

① Cut backing
Cut
0.7-cm seam
Cardboard

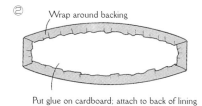

② Wrap around backing

Put glue on cardboard; attach to back of lining

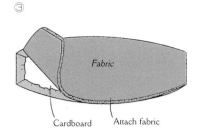

③
Fabric
Cardboard   Attach fabric

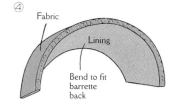

④ Fabric
Lining
Bend to fit barrette back

LOOP BROOCH AND EARRINGS

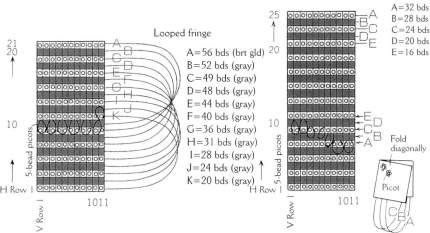

BEADS

O = Bright gold (31C) . . . . .6 g
▨ = Gray (21) . . . . .6 g

Looped fringe

A=56 bds (brt gld)
B=52 bds (gray)
C=49 bds (gray)
D=48 bds (gray)
E=44 bds (gray)
F=40 bds (gray)
G=36 bds (gray)
H=31 bds (gray)
I=28 bds (gray)
J=24 bds (gray)
K=20 bds (gray)

A=32 bds
B=28 bds
C=24 bds
D=20 bds
E=16 bds

Finished Dimensions . . . .
        (Brooch) 3.5 cm W x 5 cm L
        (Earrings) 2.5 cm W x 3.5 cm L
Tools . . . . . .Small loom, needle (medium)
Thread . . . . .Gray
Supplies . . . . .Perforated pin back (3 cm),
        earring backs
Warping method B . . . . .12 threads

Horizontal x Vert rows .(Brooch) 21 x 11
        (Earrings) 25 x 11
Fringe . . . . .Looped fringe

● INSTRUCTIONS

BROOCH: Weave piece; hide threads. Turn sideways and attach 11 strands of looped fringe.

Attach 5-bead picots in seven places at center of piece. Attach pin back (see Page 47).

EARRINGS: Weave pieces; hide threads. Fold diagonally in half, and attach five strands of looped fringe. Attach 5-bead picots in a diagonal line in seven places.

FRINGED BROOCH

FRINGE
Make 36

Finished Dimensions .5 cm W x 13 cm L
Tools . . . . .Small loom, needle (medium)
Thread . . . . .Black
SuppliesFlush perforated pin back (4.5 cm)
Warping method B . . . . .36 threads
Horizontal x Vertical rows . . . . .53 x 35
Fringe . . . . .Straight fringe

● INSTRUCTIONS

Weave Rows 1 through 39. In Row 40, decrease two beads at left and right. Continue decreasing through Row 53, forming a triangle. Hide threads. Using separate thread 80 cm long, attach fringe, starting at Row 39. Attach pin back to Row 2 (see Page 47).

BEADS

▨ = Silver (41) .8 g
✕ = Silver (21) .3 g
⊙ = Gold (36) .1 g
☐ = Black (310) 6 g
△ = Black (10C) 1 g
● = Gray (1C) .4 g

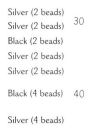

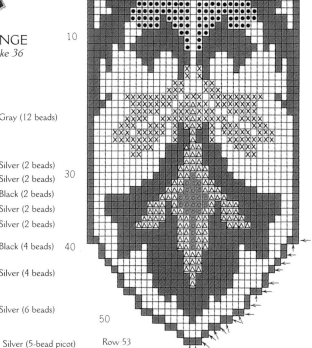

Gray (12 beads)

Silver (2 beads)
Silver (2 beads)
Black (2 beads)
Silver (2 beads)
Silver (2 beads)

Black (4 beads)

Silver (4 beads)

Silver (6 beads)

Silver (5-bead picot)

SQUARE-CUT BROOCH

Finished Dimensions .4.5 cm W x 8 cm L
Tools . . . . . .Small loom, needle (medium)
Thread . . . . .Gray
Supplies .Flush perforated pin back (6 cm)
Warping method B . . . . .30 threads
Horizontal x Vertical rows . . . . . .47 x 29

● INSTRUCTIONS

Decrease 10 beads in Row 1. Weave until you have completed Row 47, increasing and decreasing where indicated. Hide threads; attach pin back (see Page 47).

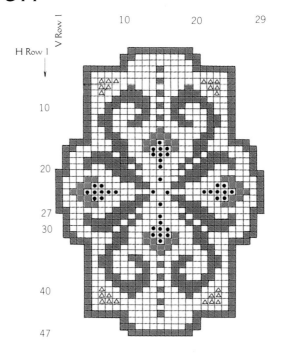

BEADS

□ = Black (10) . . . . .6 g
▨ = Silver (21) . . . . .5 g
▨ = White (201) . . .1 g
● = Gray (252) . . . . .1 g
△ = Blue (107) . . . . .1 g

RIBBON BROOCH

Finished Dimensions . . . .5 cm W x 16 cm L
Tools . . . . . . .Small loom, needle (medium)
Thread . . . . .Black
Supplies . . . . .Bow crimper
Warping method A . . . . .60 cm x 36 threads
Horizontal x Vertical rows: . . . . . . .106 x 35

● INSTRUCTIONS

Weave Rows 1 through 14, making increases at left and right. Weave Rows 15 through 53 (center). Reverse the pattern, and continue weaving from Row 52 back to Row 1. Hide threads. Gather piece at center, and attach bow crimper.

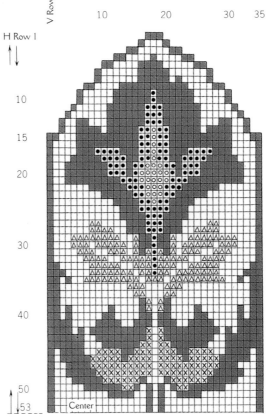

BEADS

□ = Black (310) . . .10 g
▨ = Silver (41) . . . .10 g
△ = Silver (21) . . . .2 g
○ = Silver (36) . . . .1 g
● = Black (10C) . . .2 g
✕ = Gray (1C) . . . .2 g

NECKLACE

Finished Dimensions   .2 cm W x 51 cm L
Tools . . . . .Small loom, needle (medium)
Thread . . . . .Gray
Warping method A . .90 cm x 16 threads
Horizontal x Vertical rows . . . . .270 x 14
Fringe . . . . .Straight fringe

BEADS

☐ = Silver (21) . .14g
▨ = Silver (36C) .9g
▨ = Purple (25) . .8g

● INSTRUCTIONS

Warp the loom with double thread at center. Weave from Rows 1 through 41. Starting at Row 42, weave the left and right sides separately. Use separate thread for the right side, weaving in parallel until you have completed Row 270. Join the left and right sides by hiding threads from the left side in the right side, and vice versa. Attach fringe where indicated (see Page 46).

EARRINGS

● INSTRUCTIONS

Mix the three colors of beads. For A, begin at the center with Row 1, weaving through Row 10, making increases. Begin decreasing at Row 11, forming a diamond pattern. Hide threads. Weave B in the same way. Place A on top of B as shown, and attach bead caps and earring backs.

Finished Dimensions . . . . . .3 cm x 3 cm
Tools . . . . . . .Small loom, needle (small)
Thread .Black
Supplies . . . . . .Earring backs; jump rings,
        bead tips, bead caps (two each)
Warping method B   A . . . . .20 threads
        B . . . . . .16 threads
Horizontal x Vertical rows A . . . .19 x 19
        B . . . .15 x 15

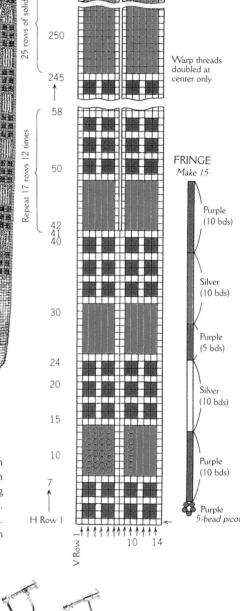

Join

270

250

245

25 rows of solid color

Warp threads
doubled at
center only

58

50

42
41
40

Repeat 17 rows 12 times

30

24

20

15

10

7

H Row 1

V Row 1   10 14

FRINGE
Make 15

Purple
(10 bds)

Silver
(10 bds)

Purple
(5 bds)

Silver
(10 bds)

Purple
(10 bds)

Purple
5-bead picot

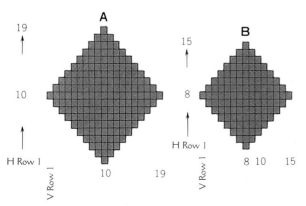

A

19

10

H Row 1

V Row 1   10   19

B

15

8

H Row 1

V Row 1   8 10   15

BEADS

Dark blue (2) . .2 g ⎫
Dark blue (325) .2 g ⎬ Mix
Gray (1) . . . . . .2 g ⎭

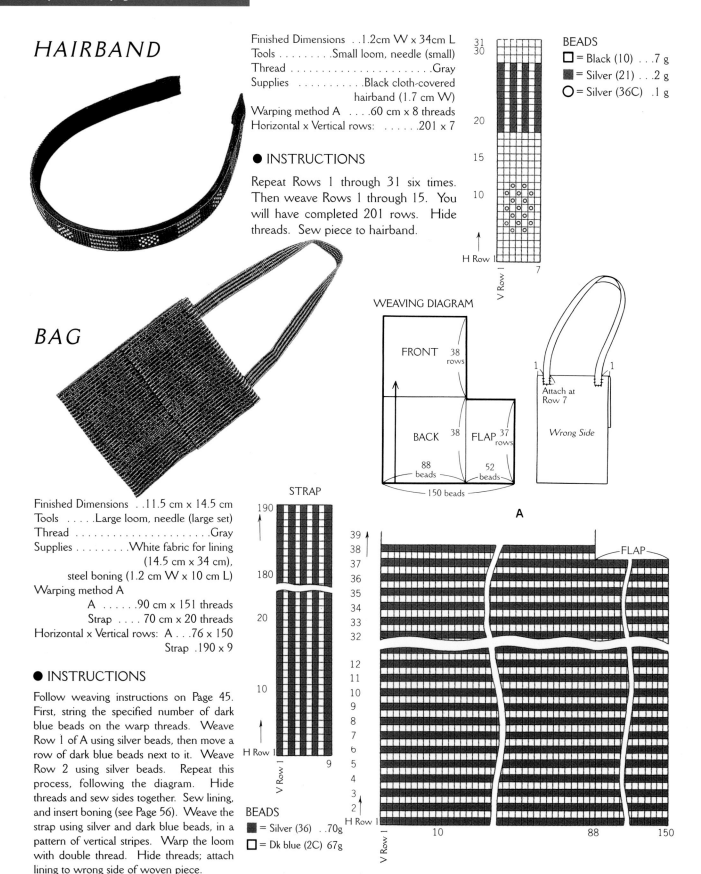

HAIRBAND

Finished Dimensions . .1.2cm W x 34cm L
Tools . . . . .Small loom, needle (small)
Thread . . . . .Gray
Supplies . . . . .Black cloth-covered
hairband (1.7 cm W)
Warping method A . . . .60 cm x 8 threads
Horizontal x Vertical rows: . . . . . .201 x 7

● INSTRUCTIONS

Repeat Rows 1 through 31 six times.
Then weave Rows 1 through 15. You
will have completed 201 rows. Hide
threads. Sew piece to hairband.

BEADS

☐ = Black (10) . . .7 g
▓ = Silver (21) . .2 g
◯ = Silver (36C) .1 g

WEAVING DIAGRAM

FRONT 38 rows

BACK 38   FLAP 37 rows

88 beads   52 beads

150 beads

A

1   1
Attach at Row 7

Wrong Side

FLAP

BAG

Finished Dimensions . .11.5 cm x 14.5 cm
Tools . . . . .Large loom, needle (large set)
Thread . . . . .Gray
Supplies . . . . .White fabric for lining
(14.5 cm x 34 cm),
steel boning (1.2 cm W x 10 cm L)
Warping method A
A . . . . . .90 cm x 151 threads
Strap . . . . 70 cm x 20 threads
Horizontal x Vertical rows: A . . .76 x 150
Strap .190 x 9

● INSTRUCTIONS

Follow weaving instructions on Page 45.
First, string the specified number of dark
blue beads on the warp threads. Weave
Row 1 of A using silver beads, then move a
row of dark blue beads next to it. Weave
Row 2 using silver beads. Repeat this
process, following the diagram. Hide
threads and sew sides together. Sew lining,
and insert boning (see Page 56). Weave the
strap using silver and dark blue beads, in a
pattern of vertical stripes. Warp the loom
with double thread. Hide threads; attach
lining to wrong side of woven piece.

STRAP

BEADS

▓ = Silver (36) . .70g
☐ = Dk blue (2C) 67g

BRACELET

Finished Dimensions . . . 1.7 cm x 16.5 cm
Tools . . . . Medium-sized loom,
                              needle (medium)
Thread . . . . Gray
Supplies . . . . Bracelet clasp
Warping method B . . . . 102 threads
Horizontal x Vertical rows: . . . . . . 101 x 6

● INSTRUCTIONS

String dark blue beads on warp threads, and
weave them, alternating with silver beads
(see Page 45). Hide threads. Attach findings
to both ends.

BEADS

☐ = Silver (36) . . . . 5 g

▨ = Dark blue (2C) . . . . 4 g

NECKLACE

Finished Dimensions . . . . 3.5 cm x 21 cm
Tools . . . . . Small loom, needle (medium)
Thread . . . . Gray
Supplies . . Necklace findings (spring ring,
                chain tag; jump rings,
                bead tips (two each)
Warping method A . . 70 cm x 20 threads
Horizontal x Vertical rows . . . . . 140 x 19

● INSTRUCTIONS

Starting after Row 1, make increases at both
sides. Weave straight from Rows 3 through
11. Remove the warp threads from the loom
temporarily, and thread the specified number
of gray beads on the warp threads. Starting
with Row 12, weave one row, then move a
row of the beads on the warp threads (see
Page 45). Repeat this process until you have
completed Row 70. Then move the center
decorative beads next to it, and weave back
from Row 70 to Row 1. Hide threads.
Attach findings (see Page 47).

BEADS

☐ = Silver (36) . . . . 14 g

▨ = Gray (1) . . . . 10 g

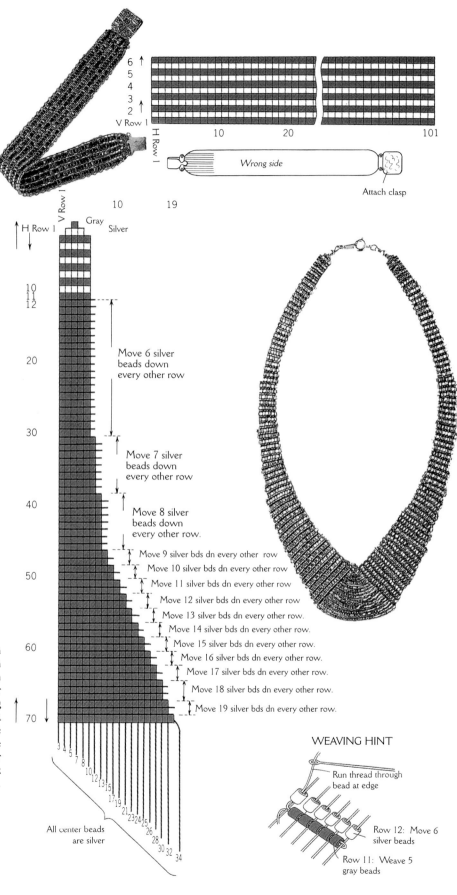

6
5
4
3
2
V Row 1

H Row 1

10   20   101

Wrong side

Attach clasp

H Row 1
V Row 1
10   19

Gray
Silver

10
11
12

20

30

40

50

60

70

Move 6 silver beads down every other row

Move 7 silver beads down every other row

Move 8 silver beads down every other row.

Move 9 silver bds dn every other row
Move 10 silver bds dn every other row
Move 11 silver bds dn every other row
Move 12 silver bds dn every other row
Move 13 silver bds dn every other row.
Move 14 silver bds dn every other row.
Move 15 silver bds dn every other row.
Move 16 silver bds dn every other row.
Move 17 silver bds dn every other row.
Move 18 silver bds dn every other row.
Move 19 silver bds dn every other row.

All center beads are silver

WEAVING HINT

Run thread through bead at edge

Row 12: Move 6 silver beads

Row 11: Weave 5 gray beads

69

OPENWORK BAG

Finished Dimensions . . .12 cm x 16.5 cm
Tools . . . . .Small loom, needle (medium)
Thread . . . . .Gray
Warping method A (Strap) . . . .
          90 cm x 10 threads (Make two)
Horizontal x Vertical rows: (Strap)231 x 4

● INSTRUCTIONS

Thread the needle and tie one bead onto the end of the thread, so that other beads won't fall off when you pick them up. Following the diagram, weave 12 rows with silver and colored beads. Repeat Rows 4 through 12. Weave backwards from Rows 9 through 1. Work 30 loops on the back, and 30 loops on the front. Join to Row 1. At the bottom of the bag, join front and back, adding five beads at a time. When you weave the straps, warp the loom with double thread. Repeat Rows 1 through 63 until you have completed 231 rows. Thread the straps through the openings near top of bag, so that it can be closed from left to right. Hide the threads from each strap in the other strap.

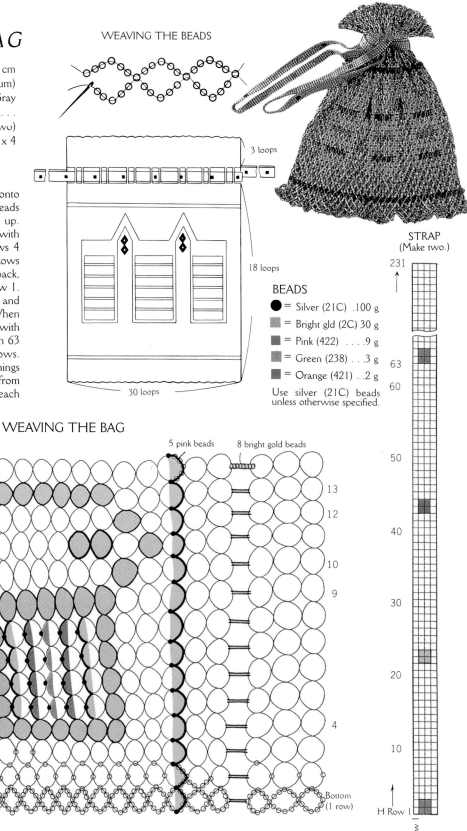

WEAVING THE BEADS

3 loops

18 loops

30 loops

BEADS

● = Silver (21C) .100 g

▦ = Bright gld (2C) 30 g

◼ = Pink (422) . . . .9 g

◾ = Green (238) . . .3 g

◾ = Orange (421) . .2 g

Use silver (21C) beads unless otherwise specified.

STRAP
(Make two.)

231

63
60

50

40

30

20

10

H Row 1

V Row 1

WEAVING THE BAG

1 gold bead   3 pink bead   5 pink beads   8 bright gold beads

V Row 1

13
12
10
9
4

Start here
Leave 10-cm end   Tie first bead

Bottom
(1 row)

EVENING PRIMROSE BARRETTE AND EARRINGS

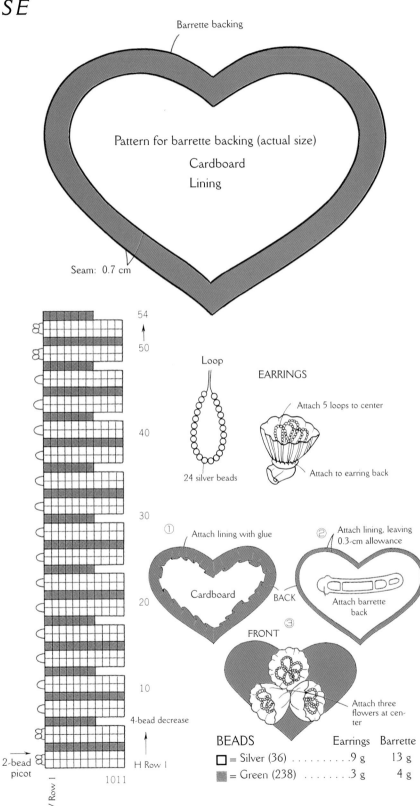

Barrette backing

Pattern for barrette backing (actual size)

Cardboard

Lining

Seam: 0.7 cm

54
↑
50

40

30

20

10

4-bead decrease
↑

H Row 1

2-bead picot

V Row 1

1011

Loop

24 silver beads

EARRINGS

Attach 5 loops to center

Attach to earring back

① Attach lining with glue

Cardboard

② Attach lining, leaving 0.3-cm allowance

BACK

Attach barrette back

FRONT ③

Attach three flowers at center

Finished Dimensions (Barrette) 8 cm x 6 cm
                                (Earrings) 3cm (diameter)
Tools . . . . .Small loom, needle (small)
Thread . . . . .Gray
Supplies . . . . . . .Perforated earring backs,
                          barrette back (6 cm),
                 black velveteen (15 cm x 15cm)
Warping method B . . . . .12 threads
Horizontal x Vertical rows: . . . . . . .54 x 11

● INSTRUCTIONS

Weave Row 1, adding 2 extra beads (picots). Weave Row 2. Weave Row 3, adding beads for picot; weave Row 4. Make a decrease on Row 5. Repeat until you have completed 54 rows. Gather the side where decreases were made, and hide threads. Form flower shape by joining piece and attaching loops at the center. Make a barrette and earrings, following the diagrams.

BEADS		Earrings	Barrette
□ = Silver (36)	. . . .	.9 g	13 g
▨ = Green (238)	. . . .	.3 g	4 g

CHERRY BARRETTE AND EARRINGS

Finished Dimensions (Barrette) 8.5 cm x 6 cm
(Pompoms) 1.8 cm (diameter)
Tools . . . . . Small loom, needle (medium)
Thread . . . . .Gray
Supplies . . . . .Barrette back (5 cm),
bead tips (three),
earring backs, jump rings (two),
small styrofoam balls (six)
Warping method B . . .(Ribbon) 12 threads
. . . .(Pompoms) 18 threads
Horizontal x Vertical rows: (Ribbon) 60 x 10
(Pompoms) 30 x 17

BEADS

☐ = Silver (36C) . . . . .4 g
■ = Purple (63) . . . . .18 g
▨ = Wine (bugle bds) . .1 pkg (3mm)
Silver (21) . . . . .2 g

● INSTRUCTIONS

To make the ribbon, weave the piece as indicated and hide threads. Gather at center and sew. To make the pompoms, weave as shown in the diagram, increasing and decreasing where indicated. Pull the warp threads, matching the darts. Place styrofoam balls inside, and sew the sides together. String gold (21) beads on thread and attach them to the four pompoms. Attach pompoms to the center of the ribbon, fasten the threads with a bead tip, and attach the barrette back.
For the earrings, make two pompoms, following the chart.

RIBBON

BARRETTE

Bead tip
24 Bds
20 Bds
16 Bds   28 Bds   Pompon

EARRING

Earring back
Jump ring
Bead tip
Pompom

POMPOM

SILK KERCHIEF BROOCH

Finished Dimensions . . .12 cm x 11.5 cm
ToolsMedium-sized loom, needle (medium)
Thread . . . . .Gray
Supplies . . . . .Bow crimper (3 cm)
Warping method A . .80 cm x 76 threads
Horizontal x Vertical rows: . . . . .41 x 75

● INSTRUCTIONS

Refer to instructions on Page 45. This piece is woven with warp and weft beads. String 40 silver (36C) beads on each warp thread. Weave the first row, and move a row of the beads on the warp threads next to it. Weave Row 2. Repeat this process until you have completed 41 rows of gold and pink beads. Hide threads. Gather a corner of the piece, and enclose it in the bow crimper.

BEADS

☐ = Silver (36C) . . . . .21 g
■ = Silver (21) . . . . .11 g
▨ = Pink (422) . . . . .11 g

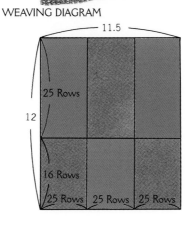

WEAVING DIAGRAM

11.5

25 Rows

12

16 Rows

25 Rows   25 Rows   25 Rows

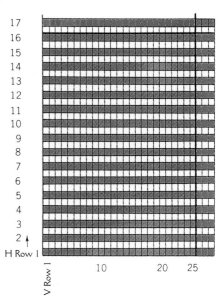

DOUBLE CHERRY BLOSSOM BAG

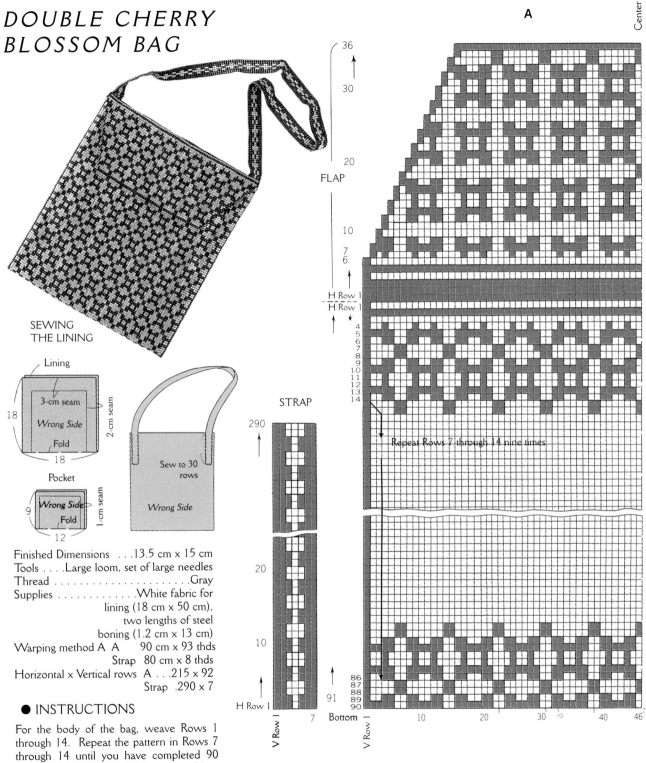

SEWING
THE LINING

Lining

3-cm seam

Wrong Side

Fold

18   18

2-cm seam

Pocket

Wrong Side

Fold

9   12

1-cm seam

STRAP

Sew to 30 rows

Wrong Side

290

20

10

H Row 1

V Row 1   7

A   Center

36
30
20

FLAP

10
7
6

H Row 1
H Row 1

4 5 6 7 8 9 10 11 12 13 14

Repeat Rows 7 through 14 nine times

86 87 88 89 90   91   Bottom

V Row 1   10   20   30   40   46

Finished Dimensions . . .13.5 cm x 15 cm
Tools . . . .Large loom, set of large needles
Thread .Gray
Supplies . . . . .White fabric for
                         lining (18 cm x 50 cm),
                         two lengths of steel
                         boning (1.2 cm x 13 cm)
Warping method A A   90 cm x 93 thds
                  Strap 80 cm x 8 thds
Horizontal x Vertical rows A . . .215 x 92
                  Strap .290 x 7

● INSTRUCTIONS

For the body of the bag, weave Rows 1 through 14. Repeat the pattern in Rows 7 through 14 until you have completed 90 rows. Then weave back from Row 91 to Row 1. Weave 36 rows for the flap, making decreases. Hide threads. Sew the lining, and hemstitch it to the front of the bag. Sew the strap to the wrong side over 30 rows, near the side seams.

BEADS

☐ = Bright gold (35) .73 g
■ = Pink (422) . . . . .80 g

73

DOUBLE CHERRY BLOSSOM BARRETTE

Finished Dinebsions . . . . .5.5 cm x 15 cm
Tools . . . . . .Small loom, needle (medium)
Thread . . . . .Gray
Supplies . . . . .Barrette back (8 cm)
Warping method A   A . . .60 cm x 66 thds
. .(Use double thread)
B . . .60 cm x 76 thds
.(Use double thread.)
Tassels: .80 cm x 4 threads
Horizontal x Vertical rows: A . . . . .90 x 32
B . . . . .94 x 37
Tassels: . . . .276 x 3
Fringe . . . . .Straight fringe

● INSTRUCTIONS

For A, weave Rows 1 through 10. Repeat pattern in Rows 3 through 10 until you have completed 90 rows. Hide threads. For B, use only purple beads, working on 37 horizontal and 94 vertical rows. Hide threads.

Place A on top of B, gather at center, and attach with thread. Weave tassels, hide threads, and attach fringe. Wind tassels around ribbon from top, and tie.

CHIGNON COVER

Finished Dimensions . . . .7 cm x 7.5 cm
Tools .Medium-sized loom, needle (med)
Thread . . . . .Gray
Supplies . . .0.5-mm-thick elastic (20 cm)
Warping method A .90 cm x 61 threads
Horizontal x Vertical rows: . . .190 x 60

● INSTRUCTIONS

Make increases and decreases at left side. Repeat Rows 1 through 38 five times, creating five peaked shapes. Pull warp threads, and sew tucks, forming a semicircle. Sew elastic to edge of piece.

BEADS

☐ =Blue (415) . . . . .28 g
▓ =Gold (34) . . . . .24 g
○ =Bright gold (31) . . . . .6 g
△ =Pink (37) . . . . .4 g

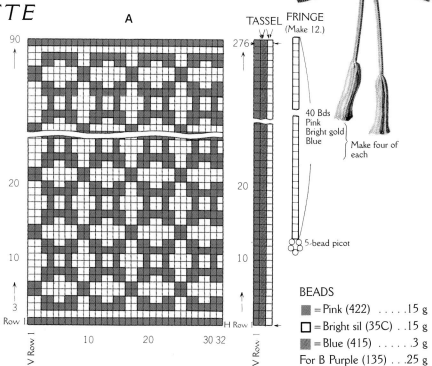

A

TASSEL   FRINGE
(Make 12.)

40 Bds
Pink
Bright gold
Blue

Make four of each

5-bead picot

BEADS

■ = Pink (422) . . . . .15 g
□ = Bright sil (35C) . .15 g
▓ = Blue (415) . . . . . .3 g
For B Purple (135) . . .25 g

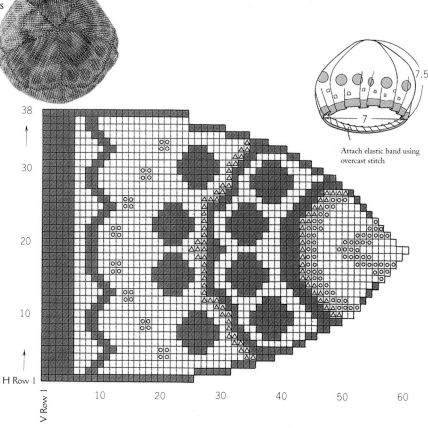

7.5

7

Attach elastic band using overcast stitch

TORTOISE SHELL BARRETTE

Finished Dimensions . . . . . . .6 cm x 14 cm
Tools . . . . . . .Small loom, needle (medium)
Thread . . . . .Gray
Supplies . . . . .Barrette back (8 cm)
Warping method A: A 80 cm x 33 threads
                   B 80 cm x 38 threads
        Blue tassel   90 cm x 4 threads
        Gold tassel   90 cm x 5 threads
Horizontal x Vertical rows: A . . . . .90 x 32
                            B . . . . .94 x 37
        Blue tassel . . . .276 x 3
        Gold tassel . . . .276 x 4
Fringe . . . . .Straight fringe

● INSTRUCTIONS

The blue ribbon and the gold ribbon are worked in exactly the same way. For A, repeat the pattern in Rows 1 through 9 nine times; hide threads. For B (use only bright gold for the blue ribbon, and red for the gold ribbon), weave 37 horizontal x 94 vertical rows. Attach fringe (6 strands for the blue ribbon, 8 for the gold ribbon) with separate thread. Place A on top of B, gather at center, and sew. Weave tassels, hide threads, and attach fringe. Attach barrette back to back of ribbon, and tie tassels on from top.

A

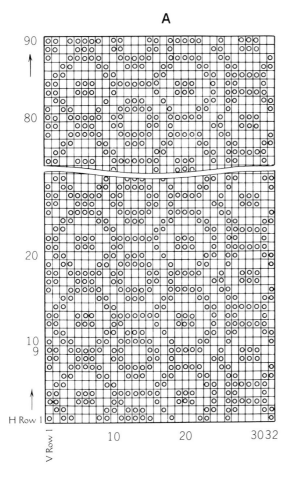

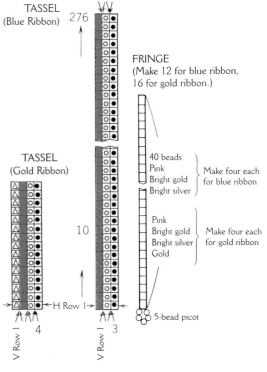

TASSEL
(Blue Ribbon)

TASSEL
(Gold Ribbon)

FRINGE
(Make 12 for blue ribbon,
16 for gold ribbon.)

40 beads
Pink
Bright gold
Bright silver } Make four each for blue ribbon

Pink
Bright gold
Bright silver
Gold } Make four each for gold ribbon

5-bead picot

BEADS

Blue ribbon		Gold ribbon	
◯ = Gold (34)	. . . . . . .15 g	◯ = Bright gold (31)	. . .15 g
☐ = Blue (415)	. . . . . . .13 g	☐ = Bright silver (35)	. . .13 g
▨ = Pink (37)	. . . . .3 g	▨ = Pink (37)	. . . . .3 g
● = Bright gold (35)	. . . .3 g	● = Rhodium (36)	. . . .3 g
B: = Bright gold (31)	. .25 g	△ = Gold (34)	. . . . .3 g
		B: = Red (103)	. . . . . .25 g

NISHIJIN BROCADE BARRETTE

Finished Dimensions . . . . .4 cm x 14 cm
Tools . . . . . . .Small loom, needle (medium)
Thread . . . . .Gray
Supplies . . . . .Barrette back (8 cm)
Warping method A   A   80 cm x 29 thds
                     B   80 cm x 26 thds
                     C   60 cm x 14 thds
Horizontal x Vertical rows: A . . . . . .90 x 28
                                 B . . . . . .70 x 25
                                 C . . . . . .25 x 13

● INSTRUCTIONS

Weave A, B, and C; hide threads. Place A on top of B, gather at center. Wrap C around barrette and attach.

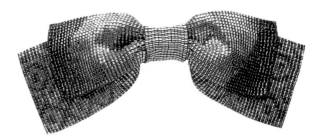

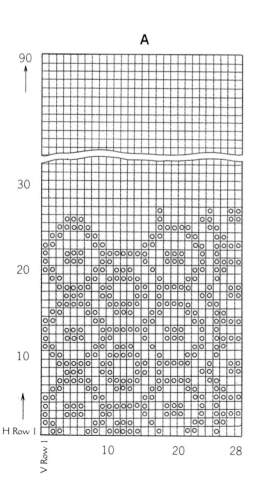

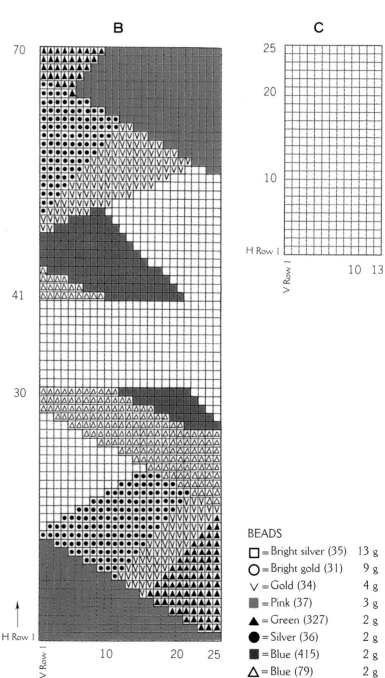

BEADS

□ = Bright silver (35)   13 g
○ = Bright gold (31)   9 g
V = Gold (34)   4 g
▨ = Pink (37)   3 g
▲ = Green (327)   2 g
● = Silver (36)   2 g
▦ = Blue (415)   2 g
△ = Blue (79)   2 g

STARDUST BARRETTE

Finished Dimensions . . .1.5 cm x 8.5 cm
Tools . . . . .Small loom, needle (medium)
Thread .Gray
Supplies . . . . . . .Barrette back (8.5 cm)
Warping method B . . . . .13 threads
Horizontal x Vertical rows . . . . .53 x 12

● INSTRUCTIONS

Weave referring to diagram; hide threads. Attach piece to barrette back, using double thread.

BEADS

□ = Silver (21) . . . . .1 g
▲ = Green (27) . . . . .1 g
○ = Bright gold (31) . . . . .1 g
▨ = Silver (41) . . . . .1 g
✕ = Blue (44) . . . . .1 g
△ = Blue (107) . . . . .1 g
● = Gray (301) . . . . .1 g
▦ = Purple (29C) . . . . .1 g

SILVERWORK COMB

Finished Dimensions . . . .9.5 cm x 3.5 cm
Tools . . . . . .Small loom, needle (medium)
Thread . . . . .Gray
Supplies . . . . .Comb (8.5 cm)
Warping method B   A . . . . .45 threads
                    B . . . . . .7 threads
Horizontal x Vertical rows: A . . . .22 x 30
                            B . . . . .20 x 6

● INSTRUCTIONS

For A, weave alternating between 2 cylindrical beads and 1 bugle bead; hide threads. Weave B; hide threads. Gather the center of A, wrap B around A, and attach to center of comb.

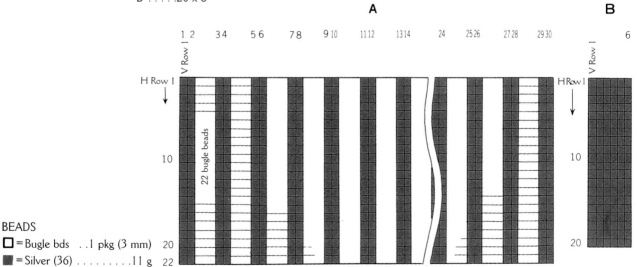

A   **B**

BEADS

□ = Bugle bds . .1 pkg (3 mm)
▨ = Silver (36) . . . . .11 g

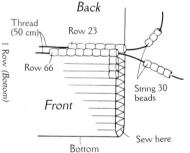

GOLD AND SILVERWORK BROOCH

Finished Dimensions . . . .
        Silver: 5 cm W x 13.5 cm L
        [Gold: 5 cm W x 12 cm L]
Tools . . . . . .Small loom, needle (medium)
Thread . . . . .Gray
Supplies . . . . . .Gold or silver bow crimper
Warping method B . . . .24 threads (90 cm)
Horizontal x Vertical rows . .Silver: 85 x 16
        [Gold: 80 x 16

*Text in brackets [ ] refers only to the gold
pin. Otherwise, the procedure is the same
as for the silver pin.*

● INSTRUCTIONS

String 24 warp threads, but do so that a two-
bead space is allowed for each bugle bead.
Pick up beads in the following order: two
cylindrical beads, one bamboo bead; repeat.
The silver ribbon is 85 rows long. For the
gold ribbon, weave 80 rows; hide threads.
Attach bow crimper to center of piece.

BEADS

☐ = Gold (21)/Silver [22] . . . . .10 g

▨ = Bugle beads 3 mm . . . . . 1 pkg gold [silver]

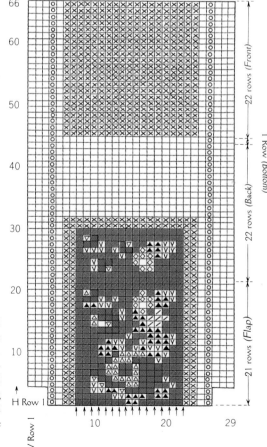

MINIATURE PURSE BROOCH WITH ROSES

Finished Dimensions .4.5 cm W x 7 cm L
Tools . . . . .Small loom, needle (medium)
Thread . . . . .Gray
Supplies . . . . .Silver ribbon pin,
        jump ring, bead tip
Warping method B . . . . .30 threads
Horizontal x Vertical rows: . . . . .66 x 29

● INSTRUCTIONS

Weave Rows 1-3, make increases at the left and
right of Row 4. Weave remainder of piece; hide
threads. Sew sides together (see Page 45).
Following directions in diagram at right for attaching the strap, cut two 50-cm lengths of thread and
run them through front and back of piece. String
30 beads onto each of the four thread ends, and
twist together (see Page 45). Attach findings (See
Page 45). Attach fringe to flap (See Page 46.)

FRINGE (16 strands)

Black (two beads)

Bright gold (3-bead picot)

ATTACHING THE STRAPS

Back

Thread (50 cm)   Row 23

Row 66

String 30 beads

Front

Bottom   Sew here

BEADS

☐ = Bright gold (31) . . . . . . .7 g

✕ = Bright silver (35) . . . . . .7 g

▨ = Black (10) . . . . .2 g

○ = Rust (22) . . . . .1 g

▨ = Red (105) . . . . .1 g

△ = Pink (106) . . . . .1 g

╱ = Purple (59) . . . . .1 g

◇ = Blue (78) . . . . .1 g

∨ = Lime (60) . . . . .1 g

▲ = Green (27) . . . . .1 g

▽ = Pink (72) . . . . .1 g

AFTERNOON BAG

Finished Dimensions . .11 cm W x 19 cm L
Tools . . . . .Medium-sized loom,
set of large needles
Thread . . . . .Gray
Supplies . . . . .Rust-colored fabric for lining
(15 cm x 34 cm),
two lengths of steel boning
(1 cm W x 9 cm L)
Warping method A . . .90 cm x 76 threads
Horizontal x Vertical rows . . . . . .222 x 75
Fringe . . . . .Straight fringe

● INSTRUCTIONS

This piece is woven from Rows 1 through 222 without increasing or decreasing. Weave the first 19 rows of the pattern, then weave Rows 20 through 30 four times. Row 88 will be the bottom of the bag, and Rows 1 through 88, the front. Weave the back and the flap in the same way, following the pattern. Cut the warp threads, leaving 15 cm on both sides. Hide 10 cm of thread in the flap, and 6 cm in the front. Run a 1-m length of thread through the bottom (Row 88), bring the thread out at both sides, and use it to sew the sides of the bag together. Attach fringe to the bottom. Weave the strap on double thread for approximately 45 cm, and attach it to the bag.

SEWING THE LINING

STRAP

FRINGE
(74 strands)

Gold (13

Red (5 bds)
Gold (3 bds)
Gold (5 bds)
Red (5-bd picot)

① LINING ③ LINING
3-cm seam
Wrong Side
Fold
② POCKET
Wrong Side Fold
④ End here Sew here
Width of woven piece minus 0.5 cm
Fold over twice, sew, and insert boning
⑤ Open seam
⑥ FLAP
Wrong Side
Hemstitch lining
Place on seam at edge and attach
25 rows
Right Side

BEADS
O = Red (423) . . . . .60 g
□ = Gold (34) . . . . . .55 g
■ = Gold (22L) . . . . .40 g

Front
Repeat Row 20 - Row 31 four times
Bottom 88
Weave back from Row 86 - Row 1
Back
Repeat Rows 20 - 31 three times, then weave Rows 80 - 87
FLAP
For the right half, weave Rows 8 through 80 from the center

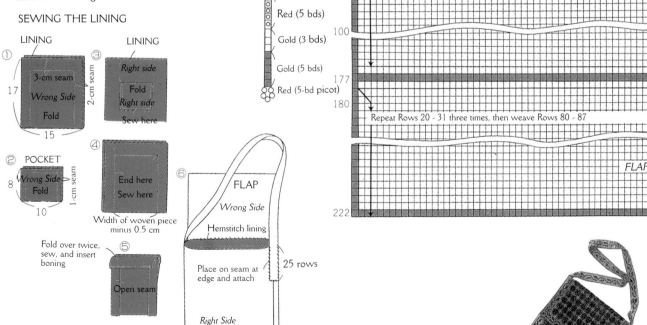

LACIS publishes and distributes books specifically related to the textile arts, focusing on the subjects of lace and lace making, costume, embroidery and hand sewing.

Other LACIS books of interest:
THE CARE AND PRESERVATION OF TEXTILES, Karen Finch & Greta Putnam
THE ART OF HAIR WORK, Mark Campbell
THE ART AND CRAFT OF RIBBON WORK, ed by Jules & Kaethe Kliot
SMOCKING AND GATHERING FOR FABRIC MANIPULATION, Nellie Weymouth Link
DRAFTING AND PATTERN DESIGNING (1926), Women's Institute of Domestic Arts
GARMENT PATTERNS, 1889, ed by Jules & Kaethe Kliot
MILLINERY FOR EVERY WOMAN, Georgina Kerr Kaye
THE TECHNIQUE OF LADIES' HAIR DRESSING (19th c.): Mark Campbell & A. Mallemont
HAUTE COUTURE EMBROIDERY: THE ART OF LESAGE, Palmer White
THE MARY FRANCES SEWING BOOK, Jane Eayre Fryer
THE MARY FRANCES KNITTING AND CROCHETING BOOK, Jane Eayre Fryer
THE MARY FRANCES HOUSEKEEPER, Jane Eayre Fryer
THE MARY FRANCES COOK BOOK, Jane Eayre Fryer
BATTENBERG AND POINT LACE, Nellie Clarke Brown
BATTENBERG LACE PATTERN BOOK, ed. Jules & Kaethe Kliot
NEEDLE LACES, BATTENBERG POINT & RETICELLA, ed. Jules & Kaethe Kliot
CROCHET: EDGINGS & INSERTIONS, Eliza A. Taylor & Belle Robinson
CROCHET: EDGINGS & MORE, ed. Jules & Kaethe Kliot
CROCHET: NOVELTIES, ed. Jules & Kaethe Kliot
CROCHET: MORE EDGINGS, ed. Jules & Kaethe Kliot
MACRAMÉ, SOURCES OF FINE KNOTTING, ed Jules & Kaethe Kliot
THE NEEDLE MADE LACES OF RETICELLA. ed Jules & Kaethe Kliot
CASALGUIDI STYLE LINEN EMBROIDERY, Effie Mitrofanis
CUTWORK, HEDEBO & BRODERIE ANGLAISE, ed Jules & Kaethe Kliot
TRADITIONAL DESIGNS IN HARDANGER EMBROIDERY, ed. Jules & Kaethe Kliot
THE ART OF SHETLAND LACE, Sarah Don
CREATING ORIGINAL HAND-KNITTED LACE, Margaret Stove
THE KNITTED LACE PATTERNS OF CHRISTINE DUCHROW V I-III. Kliot
BERLIN WORK, SAMPLERS & EMBROIDERY OF THE 19TH CENTURY. Raffaella Serena
THE MAGIC OF FREE MACHINE EMBROIDERY, Doreen Curran
DESIGNS FOR CHURCH EMBROIDERIES, Thomas Brown & Son
EMBROIDERY WITH BEADS, Angela Thompson
BEAD WORK, ed. by Jules & Kaethe Kliot
BEAD EMBROIDERY, Joan Edwards
BEAD EMBROIDERY, Valerie Campbell-Harding and Pamela Watts
INNOVATIVE BEADED JEWELRY TECHNIQUES, Gineke Root
BEADED ANIMALS IN JEWELRY, Letty Lammens and Els Scholte
CLASSIC BEADED PURSE PATTERNS, E. de Jong-Kramer
HUCK EMBROIDERY, Ondori
CREATIVE LOCKER HOOKING, Leone Peguero
TATTING: DESIGNS FROM VICTORIAN LACE CRAFT, ed.by Jules & Kaethe Kliot
THE ART OF TATTING, Katherine Hoare
TATTING WITH VISUAL PATTERNS, Mary Konior
PRACTICAL TATTING, Phyllis Sparks
NEW DIMENSIONS IN TATTING, To de Haan-van Beek
THE ART OF NETTING, Jules & Kaethe Kliot
TENERIFFE LACE, Jules & Kaethe Kliot
THE BARGELLO BOOK, Frances Salter
FLORENTINE EMBROIDERY, Barbara Muller

For a complete list of LACIS titles, write to:
LACIS
3163 Adeline Street
Berkeley, CA 94703 USA